The Next Grilleration™

George Foreman® Global G100™

Grilling Recipes from
Around the World!

D1308875

Robin Taylor Swatt

Pascoe Publishing, Inc.
Rocklin, California

Published in the United States of America by

 Pascoe Publishing, Inc.
Rocklin, California
www.pascoepublishing.com

ISBN: 978-1-929862-72-6

| 10 | 9 | 8 | 7 | 6 | 5 | 4 |
| 08 | 09 | 10 | | | | |

Printed in China

TABLE OF CONTENTS

INTRODUCTION

& *Basic Cooking Tips*

*R*eady for a savory and delicious trip around the world? Take a peek inside these pages…*Grilled Polenta with Fontina Tomato Topping, Warm Roast Beef & Mozzarella Panini, Thai Chili Beef, and Grilled Lemon-Paprika Salmon, North African Style*…each recipe is a global taste of delight!

Your George Foreman® G100™ grill is the perfect partner for your cooking adventure. Features such as the Grilling and Sauté Plates, and the Plate Position Lock Lever, offer everything you need to prepare a wide variety of new taste treats in just a matter of minutes. Think stir-frys, warm sandwiches, grilled cuts of seafood, homemade cookies, spicy barbecues, exotic flavor blends—each one prepared with healthful, good-for-you ingredients!

You'll enjoy using your George Foreman® G100™ grill for each of these recipes with a few tips in mind. First, remember to always set the Timer in order to preheat or heat the grill. Use caution when changing the hot plates, particularly if you switch plates during recipe preparation. Align the Drip Tray directly under the Lower Plate and change it if needed as foods grill. Use nonfat cooking spray on the Grilling or Sauté Plate whenever possible in place of high-fat butter or oil. Use the Sauté Plate when baking cookies, cornbread or other quick-breads. Be sure to position the Lock Lever so that the grill is either horizontal or tilted as needed for your recipe. Dishes such as eggs, pancakes and stir-frys should be prepared on the Sauté Plate in the horizontal position. Use the tilted position for grilling cuts of poultry, beef, pork or seafood. Above all, enjoy using your George Foreman® G100® grill on this delicious trip around the world!

Chapter~One

G100™
EUROPEAN & MEDITERRANEAN FLAVORS!

Lamb Souvlaki | serves 4

Serve over rice with Tzatziki Sauce *(p. 8) on the side.*

1½ lbs.	lamb, cut into bite-sized pieces
	juice of 3 lemons
1 Tbs.	extra-virgin olive oil
1 tsp.	dried oregano
1 small	red onion, grated
½ tsp.	salt
½ tsp.	freshly ground black pepper
10 –12	wooden skewers, soaked in water for 30 minutes

In a large, self-sealing plastic bag, combine the lamb, lemon juice, olive oil, oregano, onion, salt, and pepper. Refrigerate at least 3 hours or up to 8 hours.

Place the Grilling Plate on the grill and preheat to medium-high. Coat with nonfat cooking spray. Divide the lamb on the skewers and place on the grill. Close the lid and cook for 6 to 7 minutes, or until the lamb is cooked to your preference.

CALORIES:
291

TOTAL FAT:
14g

SATURATED FAT:
4g

% CAL FROM FAT:
43

CARBOHYDRATES:
5g

PROTEIN:
36g

CHOLESTEROL:
112mg

SODIUM:
407mg

Greek Beef Gyros | *serves 6*

1 lb.	thinly sliced beef sirloin
1 clove	garlic, minced
1 tsp.	fresh lemon juice
½ tsp.	dried basil
½ tsp.	dried oregano
½ tsp.	dried marjoram
½ tsp.	dried thyme
½ tsp.	dried rosemary
¼ tsp.	salt
½ tsp.	freshly ground black pepper
6 large	pita breads, cut in half
2 large	tomatoes, chopped
1 small	red onion, thinly sliced
1 cup	*Tzatziki* (recipe follows)

In a self-sealing plastic bag, combine the beef with the garlic, lemon juice, basil, oregano, marjoram, thyme, rosemary, salt, and pepper. Refrigerate for at least 1 hour or up to 8 hours.

Place the Sauté Plate in the grill and preheat to high. Coat with nonfat cooking spray. Add the beef, close the lid, and cook for 4 minutes, or until the beef is cooked to your choice. Remove from the grill. Divide the beef equally in the pita bread halves, and add the tomatoes and onions. Drizzle each pita with *Tzatziki Sauce.*

Tzatziki Sauce | *makes about 3 cups*

16 oz.	plain Greek yogurt (or strained regular yogurt)
5 cloves	garlic, minced
¾ cup	grated cucumber, excess liquid removed
2 Tbs.	fresh dill, minced
1 Tbs.	fresh lemon juice
½ tsp.	salt
½ tsp.	freshly ground black pepper

Combine all of the ingredients in a medium bowl. Refrigerate for at least 1 hour before serving.

CALORIES:
235

TOTAL FAT:
5g

SATURATED FAT:
2g

% CAL FROM FAT:
19

CARBOHYDRATES:
28g

PROTEIN:
21g

CHOLESTEROL:
47mg

SODIUM:
406mg

CALORIES:
114

TOTAL FAT:
5g

SATURATED FAT:
3g

% CAL FROM FAT:
42g

CARBOHYDRATES:
11g

PROTEIN:
6g

CHOLESTEROL:
21g

SODIUM:
465mg

Roasted Red Peppers on Grilled Halloumi Cheese | *serves 6*

2 large	red bell peppers, cored, thinly sliced
2 Tbs.	extra-virgin olive oil, divided
1 tsp.	dried oregano
1 clove	garlic, minced
¼ tsp.	salt
½ lb.	halloumi cheese, sliced into ½-inch thick pieces
1 fresh	lemon

Place the Grilling Plate on the grill and preheat to high. Coat with nonfat cooking spray. In a medium mixing bowl, combine the peppers, 1 tablespoon of olive oil, oregano, garlic, and salt.

Place the peppers on the grill, close the lid, and cook for 6 minutes, or until the peppers are soft. Remove and set aside. Brush either side of the cheese slices with the remaining olive oil. Working in batches, place the cheese on the grill, close the lid, and cook for 2 minutes. Top each slice of grilled cheese with the cooked peppers and a squeeze of lemon.

CALORIES:
163

TOTAL FAT:
11g

SATURATED FAT:
<1g

% CAL FROM FAT:
60

CARBOHYDRATES:
5g

PROTEIN:
12g

CHOLESTEROL:
0mg

SODIUM:
367mg

Potato & Feta Polpettes (Greek Potato Patties) | *serves 6*

1½ lbs.	russet potatoes, boiled, drained and peeled
6 oz.	lowfat feta cheese, crumbled
4	green onions, thinly sliced
3 Tbs.	fresh dill, chopped
1 large	egg, beaten
1 Tbs.	lemon juice
½ tsp.	salt
½ tsp.	freshly ground black pepper
2 Tbs.	extra-virgin olive oil

In a large bowl, mash the boiled potatoes while still warm. Combine with the cheese, onions, dill, egg, lemon juice, salt, and pepper until well-mixed. Cover the mixture and refrigerate for 1 hour.

Divide the potato mixture into walnut-size balls and flatten each slightly with the palm of your hand. Brush each side with a little olive oil. Place the Sauté Plate on the grill and preheat to medium-high. Coat with nonfat cooking spray. Working in batches, place the potato patties on the grill, close the lid, and cook for 7 minutes, or until heated through and golden.

CALORIES:
165

TOTAL FAT:
11g

SATURATED FAT:
<1g

% CAL FROM FAT:
63

CARBOHYDRATES:
7g

PROTEIN:
8g

CHOLESTEROL:
60mg

SODIUM:
534mg

Garlic Chicken Pita | *serves 4*

CALORIES: 285

TOTAL FAT: 8g

SATURATED FAT: <1g

% CAL FROM FAT: 24

CARBOHYDRATES: 36g

PROTEIN: 19g

CHOLESTEROL: 33mg

SODIUM: 569mg

This pita packs a garlicky punch.

3	boneless, skinless chicken breasts
1 Tbs.	extra-virgin olive oil
2 Tbs.	fresh lemon juice
4 cloves	garlic, minced
1 Tbs.	fresh oregano, chopped
¼ tsp.	salt
¼ tsp.	freshly ground black pepper
4	pita breads, halved
3 Tbs.	*Garlic Aioli* (recipe follows)
1 cup	lettuce, shredded
2	Roma tomatoes, sliced

In a self-sealing plastic bag, combine the chicken with the olive oil, lemon juice, garlic, oregano, salt, and pepper. Refrigerate for at least 1 hour or up to 8 hours.

Place the Grilling Plate on the grill and preheat to high. Coat with nonfat cooking spray. Place the chicken on the grill, close the lid, and cook for 7 to 9 minutes, or until the chicken is cooked through and no pink remains. Remove and cut into strips when cool.

To assemble the pitas, spread the interior of each half with 1 teaspoon of *Garlic Aioli*. Stuff with equal portions of chicken strips, shredded lettuce, and sliced tomatoes.

Garlic Aioli | *serves 8*

CALORIES: 104

TOTAL FAT: 10g

SATURATED FAT: 2g

% CAL FROM FAT: 88

CARBOHYDRATES: 3g

PROTEIN: <1g

CHOLESTEROL: 10mg

SODIUM: 376mg

1 cup	reduced-fat mayonnaise
6 cloves	garlic, minced
1 Tbs.	fresh lemon juice
½ tsp.	salt
½ tsp.	freshly ground black pepper

In a food processor or blender, combine the ingredients until smooth. Refrigerate. Makes about 1½ cups.

Mediterranean Grilled Chicken Salad | *serves 6*

3	boneless, skinless chicken breasts
1 clove	garlic, minced
1 Tbs.	extra-virgin olive oil
1 tsp.	fresh lemon juice
½ tsp.	dried basil
½ tsp.	dried oregano
½ tsp.	dried marjoram
½ tsp.	dried thyme
½ tsp.	dried rosemary
¼ tsp.	salt
½ tsp.	freshly ground black pepper
2	Roma tomatoes, chopped
1 small	red onion, chopped
2 med.	cucumbers, peeled and chopped
½ cup	kalamata olives, pitted and halved
3 oz.	lowfat feta cheese, crumbled

Basil & Oregano Dressing

3 Tbs.	extra-virgin olive oil
2 Tbs.	fresh lemon juice
½ tsp.	dried basil
½ tsp.	dried oregano
¼ tsp.	salt
¼ tsp.	freshly ground black pepper

In a self-sealing plastic bag, combine the chicken with the garlic, olive oil, lemon juice, basil, oregano, marjoram, thyme, rosemary, salt, and pepper. Refrigerate for at least 1 hour or up to 8 hours.

Place the Grilling Plate on the grill and preheat to high. Coat with nonfat cooking spray. Place the chicken on the grill, close the lid, and cook for 7 to 9 minutes, or until the chicken is cooked through and no pink remains. Cut the chicken into bite-sized pieces when cool. In a large bowl, combine the tomatoes, onion, cucumbers, olives, and feta cheese. Add the cooled chicken. In a small bowl, combine the dressing ingredients and toss with the salad.

CALORIES:
199

TOTAL FAT:
14g

SATURATED FAT:
<1g

% CAL FROM FAT:
65

CARBOHYDRATES:
6g

PROTEIN:
12g

CHOLESTEROL:
21mg

SODIUM:
318mg

Marianna Pita Pizza | *makes 2 servings or 4 appetizer servings*

2 med.	pita breads
2 tsp.	extra-virgin olive oil
3 Tbs.	prepared marinara sauce
3 oz.	fresh goat cheese, crumbled
½ cup	cooked spinach (defrosted from frozen), well drained of excess liquid
¼ med.	red onion, sliced
¼ cup	kalamata olives, pitted and sliced

Brush both sides of the pita bread with olive oil. Top each pita with marinara sauce, goat cheese, spinach, red onion slices, and olives.

Place the Grilling Plate on the grill and preheat to high. Coat with nonfat cooking spray. Place the pizzas on the grill without closing the lid, and grill for 4 minutes, or until the cheese has melted.

CALORIES:
196

TOTAL FAT:
10g

SATURATED FAT:
5g

% CAL FROM FAT:
46

CARBOHYDRATES:
19g

PROTEIN:
9g

CHOLESTEROL:
17mg

SODIUM:
377mg

Roasted Mussels
with Lemon & Garlic | *serves 4 as an appetizer*

CALORIES:
114

TOTAL FAT:
3g

SATURATED FAT:
<1g

% CAL FROM FAT:
21

CARBOHYDRATES:
8g

PROTEIN:
14g

CHOLESTEROL:
32mg

SODIUM:
327mg

1 lb.	well-cleaned mussels
2	shallots, sliced
3 cloves	garlic, sliced
	juice of 2 lemons
¼ cup	low-sodium chicken broth
1 Tbs.	fresh tarragon, minced
1 Tbs.	fresh flat leaf parsley, minced

Place the Sauté Plate on the grill and preheat to medium-high. Add the mussels, shallots, garlic, lemon juice, and chicken broth. Close the lid and cook for 5 minutes, or until all of the mussels have opened. Place the mussels in a large serving bowl and carefully pour the remaining sauce over the top. Garnish with tarragon and parsley.

Grilled Polenta
with Fontina Tomato Topping | *serves 10 as appetizers*

CALORIES:
313

TOTAL FAT:
10g

SATURATED FAT:
3g

% CAL FROM FAT:
28

CARBOHYDRATES:
48g

PROTEIN:
10g

CHOLESTEROL:
12mg

SODIUM:
656mg

24 oz.	tube plain polenta
2 Tbs.	extra-virgin olive oil, divided
3	Roma tomatoes, diced
1 Tbs.	fresh oregano, minced
2 cloves	garlic, minced
¼ tsp.	salt
¼ tsp.	freshly ground black pepper
2 oz.	fontina cheese, grated

Slice the polenta into ½-inch slices. Brush one side of each slice with 1 tablespoon of olive oil. In a small bowl, combine the tomatoes, oregano, garlic, salt, and pepper. Allow the flavors to marry for at least 15 minutes.

Place the Grilling Plate on the grill and preheat to high. Drizzle the remaining oil on the grill. Place the polenta in a single layer, oiled side up, on the grill. Close the lid and grill for 3 to 4 minutes, or until golden brown. Work in batches, if necessary. Top each polenta round with fontina cheese and the diced tomato topping.

Fresh Figs with Goat Cheese & Prosciutto | *serves 6 as an appetizer*

12	fresh figs, stems removed
4 oz.	goat cheese, cut into 12 chunks
6 slices	prosciutto, sliced in half lengthwise
2 Tbs.	honey
12	food picks

Slice each fig open, cutting down from the top without cutting all the way through. Place one piece of cheese in each fig and wrap the fig in prosciutto, using a pick to keep the bundle together.

Place the Grilling Plate on the grill and preheat to high. Coat with nonfat cooking spray. Place the figs on the grill, close the lid, and let cook for 2 to 3 minutes, or until the cheese has melted. Remove from the grill and drizzle with honey.

CALORIES:
290

TOTAL FAT:
14g

SATURATED FAT:
5g

% CAL FROM FAT:
42

CARBOHYDRATES:
30g

PROTEIN:
14g

CHOLESTEROL:
20mg

SODIUM:
569mg

Roasted Tomato Bruschetta | *serves 7 as an appetizer*

6	Roma tomatoes, cut in half widthwise
2 cloves	garlic, minced
2 Tbs.	extra-virgin olive oil
3 Tbs.	fresh basil, sliced into a chiffonade
2 Tbs.	capers
½ tsp.	freshly ground black pepper
14 slices	ciabatta (or other rustic bread)
	extra-virgin olive oil

Place the Grilling Plate on the grill and preheat to high. Coat with nonfat cooking spray. Seed the tomatoes by squeezing each half and allowing the seeds and juice to run out. Place the tomato halves on the Grilling Plate, cut side down, and close the lid. Cook for 3 minutes or until the tomatoes have softened. Remove the tomatoes from the grill, cool and chop finely. Combine with the olive oil, basil, capers and pepper in a medium bowl and set aside to meld the flavors.

Brush each slice of bread with a little olive oil and place on the grill. Close the lid and grill for 2 to 3 minutes, or until the bread is golden. Remove from the grill and top with the tomato mixture.

CALORIES:
292

TOTAL FAT:
6g

SATURATED FAT:
<1g

% CAL FROM FAT:
17

CARBOHYDRATES:
50g

PROTEIN:
10g

CHOLESTEROL:
0mg

SODIUM:
570mg

Grilled Vegetable Tapas | *serves 8*

CALORIES:
130

TOTAL FAT:
10g

SATURATED FAT:
1g

% CAL FROM FAT:
69

CARBOHYDRATES:
8g

PROTEIN:
2g

CHOLESTEROL:
7mg

SODIUM:
327mg

2 med.	zucchini, cut lengthwise into ¼-inch slices
2 med.	yellow squash, cut lengthwise into ¼-inch slices
1 large	red bell pepper, cored and seeded, cut into 1-inch spears
½ lb.	asparagus, cleaned and trimmed
2 Tbs.	extra-virgin olive oil, divided
2 cloves	garlic, minced
¼ tsp.	salt
¼ tsp.	freshly ground black pepper
1 cup	*Garlic Aioli* (recipe on page 10)

In a large bowl, combine the vegetables, olive oil, garlic, salt, and pepper, until the vegetables are well-coated. Place the Grilling Plate on the grill, preheat to high, and coat with nonfat cooking spray. Working in batches, place the vegetables on the preheated grill, close the lid, and grill for 4 minutes, or until the vegetables are slightly softened. Remove from the grill and set aside. Place a bowl of *Garlic Aioli* in the middle of a serving platter and arrange the vegetables around the aioli.

Easy Spanish Chorizo Tapas | *serves 8 as appetizers*

CALORIES:
508

TOTAL FAT:
31g

SATURATED FAT:
7g

% CAL FROM FAT:
56

CARBOHYDRATES:
34g

PROTEIN:
22g

CHOLESTEROL:
64mg

SODIUM:
1029mg

1 lb.	medium chorizo links, casings removed and cut into ½-inch slices
4 med.	tomatoes, cut into wedges
½ lb.	Spanish manchego cheese
1 cup	assorted olives
1 loaf	crusty French bread, cut into ½-inch slices
2 Tbs.	extra-virgin olive oil

Place the Grilling Plate on the grill and preheat to high. Coat with nonfat cooking spray. Place the chorizo slices on the grill, close the lid, and cook for 3 minutes. Remove and place on a serving platter. Arrange the tomato wedges, cheese, and olives around the chorizo.

Brush the bread slices with oil and place on the grill. Close the lid and grill on high heat for 3 minutes, or until golden. Serve on the side with the platter of tapas.

Asparagus Bundles with Ham & Cheese | *serves 4*

4 oz.	lowfat Swiss cheese, cut into 4 spears
12	spears asparagus, cleaned and trimmed
4 slices	Parma ham or prosciutto
1 Tbs.	extra-virgin olive oil
	food picks

To create the bundles, surround 1 spear of cheese with 3 asparagus spears, and wrap with the Parma ham, using food picks to keep the edges together. Drizzle with olive oil. Create 4 bundles.

Place the Grilling Plate on the grill, preheat to high, and coat with nonfat cooking spray. Place the bundles on the grill, close the lid, and cook for 4 minutes. Remove from the grill and serve.

CALORIES:
221

TOTAL FAT:
16g

SATURATED FAT:
3g

% CAL FROM FAT:
63

CARBOHYDRATES:
2g

PROTEIN:
18g

CHOLESTEROL:
17mg

SODIUM:
583mg

Basil Turkey Skewers | *serves 5*

2	turkey breast tenderloins (about 1½ lbs.), cut into bite-sized pieces
4 Tbs.	prepared pesto sauce, divided
½ tsp.	salt
2 med.	zucchini, cut into ½-inch slices
2 med.	yellow squash, cut into ½-inch slices
20	cherry tomatoes
10	wooden skewers, soaked in water for 30 minutes

In a large self-sealing plastic bag, combine the turkey pieces, 2 tablespoons of pesto sauce, and salt until the turkey is well-coated. Refrigerate for at least 1 hour or up to 8 hours. In a separate container, combine the zucchini and squash slices with the remaining pesto sauce and set aside.

Place the Grilling Plate on the grill and preheat to medium-high. Coat with nonfat cooking spray. Evenly dividing the ingredients, alternate the turkey pieces, cherry tomatoes, zucchini, and squash on the 10 bamboo skewers. Place the skewers on the grill, close the lid and cook for 7 to 9 minutes, or until the turkey is cooked through and no pink remains.

CALORIES:
295

TOTAL FAT:
11g

SATURATED FAT:
1g

% CAL FROM FAT:
31

CARBOHYDRATES:
15g

PROTEIN:
42g

CHOLESTEROL:
98mg

SODIUM:
451mg

Spanish Tortilla | *serves 6 as appetizers*

1 Tbs.	extra-virgin olive oil
1 cup	Yukon gold potatoes, sliced and cooked until tender
½ small	yellow onion, peeled and sliced
5 large	eggs, beaten (or equivalent egg substitute)
½ tsp.	fresh thyme leaves, chopped
¼ cup	*Roasted Red Pepper Aioli* (recipe follows)

Place the Sauté Plate on the grill and preheat to medium-high. Coat with nonfat cooking spray. Place the olive oil, sliced potatoes, and onion in the Sauté Plate, close the lid, and cook for 4 minutes, stirring occasionally. When the onion is translucent, pour the beaten eggs over the potato-onion mixture, sprinkle with thyme, and cook an additional 2 minutes, or until set. Using a plastic spatula, remove from the plate. Serve warm or at room temperature with the *Roasted Red Pepper Aioli*.

CALORIES: 110
TOTAL FAT: 7g
SATURATED FAT: 1g
% CAL FROM FAT: 57
CARBOHYDRATES: 6g
PROTEIN: 6g
CHOLESTEROL: 177mg
SODIUM: 160mg

Roasted Red Pepper Aioli | *makes about 1 1/2 cups*

1 cup	reduced-fat mayonnaise
3 cloves	garlic, minced
3 oz.	jar roasted red peppers
1 Tbs.	fresh lemon juice
½ tsp.	salt
½ tsp.	freshly ground black pepper

In a food processor or blender, combine the aioli ingredients until smooth. Refrigerate.

CALORIES: 75
TOTAL FAT: 3g
SATURATED FAT: 0g
% CAL FROM FAT: 32
CARBOHYDRATES: 12g
PROTEIN: <1g
CHOLESTEROL: 0mg
SODIUM: 624mg

Prawn Skewers with Sun-dried Tomato Walnut Pesto | *serves 4*

1½ oz.	sun-dried tomatoes, reconstituted with boiling water
1 cup	fresh basil leaves, chopped
¼ cup	toasted walnuts, chopped
2 Tbs.	extra-virgin olive oil
2 Tbs.	water
2 tsp.	balsamic vinegar
2 cloves	garlic, chopped
¼ tsp.	salt
¼ tsp.	freshly ground black pepper
1½ lbs.	medium prawns, peeled and deveined
8-10	wooden skewers, soaked in water for 30 minutes

In a blender or food processor, make the pesto by combining the sun-dried tomatoes, basil, walnuts, oil, water, vinegar, garlic, salt, and pepper until well-blended. In a self-sealing plastic bag, combine half of the pesto sauce with the prawns and refrigerate for 1 to 2 hours.

Prepare the Grilling Plate on the grill and preheat the grill to high. Coat with nonfat cooking spray. Place the prawns on the skewers and place each skewer on the grill. Baste with the remaining pesto sauce. Close the lid and grill for 3 minutes, or until the prawns are cooked through.

CALORIES:
318

TOTAL FAT:
16g

SATURATED FAT:
1g

% CAL FROM FAT:
45

CARBOHYDRATES:
6g

PROTEIN:
37g

CHOLESTEROL:
259mg

SODIUM:
426mg

Croque Monsieur Sandwich | *serves 1*

2 oz.	lowfat baked ham, thinly sliced
1 oz.	Gruyere cheese, grated
2 slices	white sandwich bread
1 tsp.	lowfat butter-flavored spread or margarine

Form a sandwich by placing the ham and cheese inside the bread slices. Spread the margarine or spread on the outside of each piece of bread.

Place the Sauté Plate on the grill and preheat to medium-high. Coat with nonfat cooking spray. Place the sandwich on the grill, close the lid, and cook for 2 minutes, or until the cheese has melted and the bread is golden brown.

CALORIES:
325

TOTAL FAT:
9g

SATURATED FAT:
7g

% CAL FROM FAT:
38

CARBOHYDRATES:
29g

PROTEIN:
22g

CHOLESTEROL:
57mg

SODIUM:
882mg

Garlic Toasts with Brie & Walnuts | *serves 4 as appetizers*

CALORIES:
335

TOTAL FAT:
17g

SATURATED FAT:
6g

% CAL FROM FAT:
44

CARBOHYDRATES:
35g

PROTEIN:
12g

CHOLESTEROL:
28mg

SODIUM:
524mg

8 slices	baguette, cut into ½-inch thick slices
1 Tbs.	extra-virgin olive oil
2 cloves	garlic, peeled
4 oz.	brie cheese, cut into 8 slices, at room temperature
3 Tbs.	sweetened, dried cranberries
3 Tbs.	toasted walnuts, chopped

Brush the bread slices with olive oil. Rub each with the garlic cloves and discard the cloves. Place the Grilling Plate on the grill and preheat to medium-high. Coat with nonfat cooking spray. Place the bread slices on the grill, close the lid, and grill for 2 minutes, or until the bread is golden. Top each bread slice with a slice of brie and let sit on the grill until slightly melted, about 2 minutes. Remove from the grill and arrange on a serving platter. Garnish with cranberries and walnuts.

Warm Roast Beef & Mozzarella Panini | *serves 4*

CALORIES:
310

TOTAL FAT:
11g

SATURATED FAT:
3g

% CAL FROM FAT:
31

CARBOHYDRATES:
32g

PROTEIN:
21g

CHOLESTEROL:
42mg

SODIUM:
1040mg

8 slices	crusty bread or 4 baguette-style sandwich rolls
1 Tbs.	extra-virgin olive oil
8 slices	roast beef (about 1 oz. each)
6 oz.	jar of roasted red peppers, drained and cut into thin strips
2 oz.	part-skim mozzarella cheese, cut into 4 slices

Spread the exterior of the bread slices or sandwich rolls with the olive oil. Form 4 sandwiches using the roast beef, roasted red peppers, and cheese. Place the Grilling Plate on the grill and preheat to medium-high. Coat with nonfat cooking spray. Place the sandwiches on the grill, close the lid, and cook for 2 to 3 minutes, or until the bread is golden and the cheese has melted.

Chicken Pesto Panini | *serves 4*

3	boneless, skinless chicken breasts
1 Tbs.	extra-virgin olive oil, divided
2 Tbs.	fresh lemon juice
4 cloves	garlic, minced
1 Tbs.	fresh parsley, chopped
¼ tsp.	salt
¼ tsp.	freshly ground black pepper
8 slices	crusty bread (or 4 sandwich rolls)
⅛ cup	prepared basil pesto
4 Tbs.	reduced-fat mayonnaise
6 oz.	jar roasted red peppers, drained and cut into thin strips
2 oz.	part-skim provolone cheese, cut into 4 slices

In a self-sealing plastic bag, combine the chicken with 1 tablespoon of the oil, lemon juice, garlic, parsley, salt, and pepper. Refrigerate for at least 1 hour or up to 8 hours.

Place the Grilling Plate on the grill and preheat to high. Coat with nonfat cooking spray. Place the chicken on the grill, close the lid, and cook for 7 to 9 minutes, or until the chicken is cooked through and no pink remains. Remove the chicken and slice into strips when cool.

Spread the exterior of the bread slices with the remaining oil. In a small bowl, combine the basil pesto and mayonnaise and spread over the interior of each slice. Form sandwiches filled with the chicken strips, red peppers, and provolone cheese. Place the Grilling Plate on the grill and preheat to medium-high. Coat with nonfat cooking spray. Place the sandwiches on the grill, close the lid, and cook for 2 to 3 minutes, or until the bread is golden brown and the cheese has melted.

CALORIES:
377

TOTAL FAT:
13g

SATURATED FAT:
4g

% CAL FROM FAT:
40

CARBOHYDRATES:
42g

PROTEIN:
23g

CHOLESTEROL:
39mg

SODIUM:
1390mg

Bruschetta Caprese | *serves 4*

8 slices	baguette or rustic bread, cut into ½-inch thick slices
1 Tbs.	extra-virgin olive oil
8 slices	Roma tomato
8 fresh	basil leaves
4 oz.	part-skim fresh mozzarella, cut into 8 slices
	salt and pepper to taste

Brush the bread slices with olive oil. Place the Grilling Plate on the grill and preheat to medium-high. Coat with nonfat cooking spray. Place the bread slices on the grill, close the lid, and grill for 2 minutes, or until the bread is golden. Remove from the grill and place on a serving platter. Top each bread slice with a slice of fresh mozzarella. Layer each with the basil and a slice of tomato. Season with salt and pepper to taste.

CALORIES:
269

TOTAL FAT:
10g

SATURATED FAT:
4g

% CAL FROM FAT:
35

CARBOHYDRATES:
30g

PROTEIN:
13g

CHOLESTEROL:
15mg

SODIUM:
547mg

Zucchini & Sweet Potato Latkes | *serves 6*

CALORIES:
138

TOTAL FAT:
4g

SATURATED FAT:
1g

% CAL FROM FAT:
27

CARBOHYDRATES:
19g

PROTEIN:
6g

CHOLESTEROL:
108mg

SODIUM:
380mg

4 med.	zucchini, grated
1 med.	sweet potato, peeled and grated
1 small	white onion, peeled and grated
3 large	eggs, beaten (or equivalent egg substitute)
2 Tbs.	fresh flat leaf parsley, minced
½ cup	flour
1 Tbs.	baking powder
½ tsp.	salt
½ tsp.	freshly ground black pepper
	vegetable oil
	lowfat sour cream for garnish

In a large bowl, combine the zucchini, sweet potato, and onion. Squeeze out any excess liquid and discard. Add the eggs, parsley, flour, baking powder, salt, and pepper to the grated vegetables and mix well to combine.

Place the Sauté Plate on the grill and preheat to medium. Coat with nonfat cooking spray and drizzle with a small bit of oil. Working in batches, drop the vegetable mixture by tablespoons onto the Sauté Plate and cook for 2 minutes. Using a plastic spatula, flip each latke over and cook for another 2 minutes, or until lightly brown. Repeat with the remaining latkes. Serve with sour cream.

Vegetable Ratatouille | *serves 4*

CALORIES:
161

TOTAL FAT:
11g

SATURATED FAT:
<1g

% CAL FROM FAT:
57

CARBOHYDRATES:
16g

PROTEIN:
3g

CHOLESTEROL:
0mg

SODIUM:
302mg

1 med.	zucchini, chopped
1 med.	eggplant, cubed
1 small	red onion, chopped
1 large	red bell pepper, chopped
3	Roma tomatoes, diced
2 cloves	garlic, minced
½ tsp.	dried thyme
½ tsp.	dried oregano
½ tsp.	dried basil
1 tsp.	fresh flat leaf parsley
½ tsp.	salt
½ tsp.	freshly ground black pepper
3 Tbs.	extra-virgin olive oil

In a large mixing bowl, combine all of the ingredients.

Place the Sauté Plate on the grill and preheat to medium-high. Coat with nonfat cooking spray. Place the vegetable mixture onto the Sauté Plate and cook for 5 to 6 minutes with the lid open. Stir occasionally and cook until the vegetables have softened. Close the lid and cook an additional 3 minutes or until cooked to your preference. Serve while warm.

G100™

ASIAN FLAVORS!

Chapter-Two

Nua Pad Prik (Thai Chili Beef) | *makes 4 servings*

1 lb.	beef tenderloin, thinly sliced
2 cloves	garlic, minced
1	jalapeño pepper, seeded and minced
	salt and pepper to taste
2 Tbs.	fish sauce
1 Tbs.	oyster sauce
1 tsp.	brown sugar, packed
1 large	red bell pepper, thinly sliced
1 med.	yellow onion, thinly sliced
2 Tbs.	fresh cilantro, chopped

Combine the beef, garlic, jalapeño pepper, salt, and pepper in a bowl and refrigerate for 30 minutes. Place the Sauté Plate on the grill and preheat the grill to high. Coat with nonfat cooking spray. Combine the fish sauce, oyster sauce, and sugar in a small bowl and set aside.

Place the bell pepper and yellow onion on the Sauté Plate and grill for 1 minute. Add the marinated beef, close the lid and grill for 5 minutes. Add the fish sauce mixture and stir to combine. Cook for an additional 1 minute. Garnish with cilantro and serve over rice or noodles.

CALORIES:
206

TOTAL FAT:
8g

SATURATED FAT:
3g

% CAL FROM FAT:
37

CARBOHYDRATES:
7g

PROTEIN:
25g

CHOLESTEROL:
70mg

SODIUM:
857mg

Chicken Yakitori | *serves 4*

The Japanese version of chicken barbecue, this dish is a popular "quick bite" in Japan.

CALORIES: 175
TOTAL FAT: 1g
SATURATED FAT: <1g
% CAL FROM FAT: 8
CARBOHYDRATES: 20g
PROTEIN: 20g
CHOLESTEROL: 31mg
SODIUM: 2064mg

1 cup	low-sodium soy sauce
3 Tbs.	rice vinegar
2 Tbs.	sugar
3	boneless, skinless chicken breasts, cut into bite-sized pieces
12	green onions, green tops removed, cut into 1½-inch batons
2 Tbs.	toasted sesame seeds
10	wooden skewers, soaked in water for 30 minutes

In a small bowl, combine the soy sauce, rice vinegar, and sugar. Reserve ¼ cup of the marinade and pour the remaining marinade into a self-sealing plastic bag. Add the chicken pieces and refrigerate for at least 1 hour or up to 8 hours.

Place the Grilling Plate on the grill and preheat the grill to medium. Coat with nonfat cooking spray. Thread the chicken and green onions on the skewers and place on the grill. Close the lid and grill for 3 minutes. Open the lid, drizzle the reserved marinade over the chicken, and close the grill. Grill for 4 minutes, or until the chicken is cooked through with no pink remaining. Garnish each skewer with sesame seeds before serving.

Spicy Asian-style Ahi Tuna | *serves 4*

CALORIES: 199
TOTAL FAT: 2g
SATURATED FAT: <1g
% CAL FROM FAT: 9
CARBOHYDRATES: 3g
PROTEIN: 41g
CHOLESTEROL: 77mg
SODIUM: 340mg

2 Tbs.	low-sodium soy sauce
1 tsp.	fresh ginger, minced
1 tsp.	honey
1 tsp.	Asian chilie paste
1 Tbs.	fresh cilantro, minced
4 6 oz.	Ahi tuna steaks

Place the soy sauce, ginger, honey, chilie paste, and cilantro in a self-sealing plastic bag. Add the tuna steaks and refrigerate for 1 hour. Place the Grilling Plate on the grill and preheat to high. Coat with nonfat cooking spray. Place the Ahi steaks on the grill, close the lid, and grill for 4 minutes.

Thai Chicken Sate
with Lime & Garlic Marinade | *serves 4*

Lime & Garlic Marinade
2 cloves   garlic, finely minced
1-inch   piece fresh ginger, finely grated
1 Tbs.   fresh lime juice
2 Tbs.   low-sodium soy sauce
1 Tbs.   honey

3   boneless, skinless chicken breasts, each
cut into 4 long strips
12   wooden skewers, soaked in water for
30 minutes

Peanut Sauce
¼ cup   reduced-fat creamy peanut butter
½ tsp.   crushed red pepper flakes
¼ cup   warm water
1 Tbs.   fresh lime juice
1 tsp.   brown sugar, packed
1 Tbs.   fresh cilantro, minced

Combine the marinade ingredients in a large, self-sealing plastic bag and add the chicken strips. Refrigerate for at least 1 hour or up to 8 hours.

Place the Grilling Plate on the grill and preheat the grill to high. Coat with nonfat cooking spray. Remove the chicken from the marinade and thread each piece onto a skewer. Place on the grill, close the lid and grill for 5 to 7 minutes, or until the chicken is cooked through and no pink remains.

Meanwhile, whisk together the *Peanut Sauce* ingredients in a small bowl. Remove the chicken from the grill and drizzle the sauce over each piece before serving.

CALORIES: 191
TOTAL FAT: 7g
SATURATED FAT: 2g
% CAL FROM FAT: 35
CARBOHYDRATES: 15g
PROTEIN: 17g
CHOLESTEROL: 33mg
SODIUM: 377mg

Grilled Sesame Bok Choy | *serves 2*

2 med.   bok choy (or 4 baby bok choy), cut in
half lengthwise, and well-rinsed
1 tsp.   extra-virgin olive oil
salt and pepper to taste
1 tsp.   toasted sesame oil
1 tsp.   toasted sesame seeds

Place the Grilling Plate on the grill and preheat to high. Coat with nonfat cooking spray. In a medium bowl, drizzle the bok choy halves with olive oil and season with salt and pepper. Place the bok choy, cut-side down, on the grill. Close the lid and grill for 3 minutes. Remove, drizzle with sesame oil and sprinkle with toasted sesame seeds. Serve while warm.

CALORIES: 55
TOTAL FAT: 5g
SATURATED FAT: 0g
% CAL FROM FAT: 71
CARBOHYDRATES: 2g
PROTEIN: 2g
CHOLESTEROL: 0mg
SODIUM: 47mg

Teriyaki Tofu | *serves 3*

CALORIES:
201

TOTAL FAT:
4g

SATURATED FAT:
0g

% CAL FROM FAT:
17

CARBOHYDRATES:
31g

PROTEIN:
13g

CHOLESTEROL:
0mg

SODIUM:
1396mg

14 oz.	block firm tofu, drained
½ cup	low-sodium soy sauce
¼ cup	sugar
1 Tbs.	dark molasses
1 clove	garlic, minced
1-inch	piece fresh ginger, minced

Cut the tofu crosswise into 6 slices. Arrange in one layer on a triple layer of paper towels and top with another triple layer of towels. Weight the tofu with a shallow baking pan or baking sheet and let stand 2 minutes. Drain any excess moisture. Repeat the process twice with dry paper towels.

In a small bowl, combine the remaining ingredients. Place the tofu in a shallow dish and pour the teriyaki sauce over the tofu. Let marinate for 30 minutes. Place the Grilling Plate on the grill and preheat to high. Coat grill with nonfat cooking spray. Place the tofu slices on the grill. Close the lid and grill for 2 minutes. Drizzle any remaining marinade over the tofu before serving.

Lime & Soy-Glazed Eggplant | *serves 4*

CALORIES:
78

TOTAL FAT:
2g

SATURATED FAT:
<1g

% CAL FROM FAT:
16

CARBOHYDRATES:
15g

PROTEIN:
3g

CHOLESTEROL:
0mg

SODIUM:
259mg

2 Tbs.	low-sodium soy sauce
1 Tbs.	fresh lime juice
1 tsp.	toasted sesame oil
2 med.	eggplants, sliced into ½-inch slices

Place the Grilling Plate on the grill and preheat to high. Coat with nonfat cooking spray. Combine the soy sauce, lime juice, and sesame oil in a small bowl. Brush the mixture over the eggplant slices, coating each side. Place the eggplant slices on the grill, close the lid and cook for 3 to 4 minutes, or until the eggplant is tender.

Orange & Soy Glazed Salmon | *serves 4*

¼ cup	low-sodium soy sauce
2 Tbs.	fresh orange juice
2 Tbs.	honey
1 Tbs.	Dijon mustard
1 Tbs.	fresh ginger, minced
¼ tsp.	crushed red pepper flakes
4 6 oz.	boneless pink salmon fillets

In a small bowl, whisk together the soy sauce, orange juice, honey, mustard, ginger, and pepper flakes. Reserve 2 tablespoons of the marinade and set aside. Place the salmon fillets in a self-sealing plastic bag and pour the marinade over the salmon. Refrigerate for 1 hour.

Place the Grilling Plate on the grill and preheat to high. Coat with nonfat cooking spray. Place the fillets on the heated grill. Close the lid and grill for 4 minutes, or until the salmon is cooked through. Drizzle the reserved marinade over each fillet just before serving.

CALORIES:
254

TOTAL FAT:
6g

SATURATED FAT:
1g

% CAL FROM FAT:
23

CARBOHYDRATES:
11g

PROTEIN:
36g

CHOLESTEROL:
88mg

SODIUM:
705mg

Vegetable Yakisoba (Japanese Fried Noodles) | *makes 4 servings*

3 Tbs.	low-sodium soy sauce
3 Tbs.	water
3 Tbs.	sugar
1 tsp.	toasted sesame oil
1 clove	garlic, minced
1-inch	piece fresh ginger, minced
1 large	carrot, peeled and julienned
1 med.	yellow onion, peeled and sliced
3 spears	asparagus, cut into 1-inch pieces
¼ cup	green cabbage, shredded
1 cup	frozen peas
8 oz.	pkg. fresh yakisoba noodles, rinsed (or use fresh fettuccini noodles)

Place the Sauté Plate on the grill and preheat to high. While grill is heating, combine the soy sauce, water, and sugar in a small bowl and set aside. Sauté the sesame oil, garlic, and ginger for 1 minute, stirring once. Add the carrot, onion, asparagus, cabbage, and frozen peas, and cook and stir for another 3 minutes. Add the noodles and soy sauce mixture, mix well, and close the lid, cooking for another 3 minutes.

CALORIES:
300

TOTAL FAT:
2g

SATURATED FAT:
<1g

% CAL FROM FAT:
5

CARBOHYDRATES:
64g

PROTEIN:
12g

CHOLESTEROL:
0mg

SODIUM:
879mg

Moo Goo Gai Pan
Chinese Chicken & Mushroom Stir-fry | *serves 4*

CALORIES:
128

TOTAL FAT:
3g

SATURATED FAT:
<1g

% CAL FROM FAT:
24

CARBOHYDRATES:
10g

PROTEIN:
14g

CHOLESTEROL:
33mg

SODIUM:
343mg

Soy & Lemon Marinade

2 Tbs.	low-sodium soy sauce
2 tsp.	fresh lemon juice
½ tsp.	toasted sesame oil
1 Tbs.	cornstarch
1 tsp.	vegetable oil
3	boneless, skinless chicken breasts, cut into thin strips
1 cup	fresh button mushrooms, halved
½ cup	canned bamboo shoots, drained
½ cup	canned water chestnuts, drained
1 clove	garlic, minced
4	green onions, bias-cut into 1-inch pieces
½-inch	fresh ginger, minced

Oyster Sauce

¼ cup	low-sodium chicken broth
2 tsp.	cornstarch
2 Tbs.	oyster sauce

Combine the *Soy & Lemon Marinade* ingredients and the chicken in a self-sealing plastic bag. Refrigerate for at least 1 hour or up to 8 hours.

Place the Sauté Plate on the grill and preheat to high. Drizzle the oil on the Sauté Plate and add the chicken strips. Cook for 1 minute. Add the mushrooms, bamboo shoots, water chestnuts, garlic, green onions and ginger. Close the lid and cook for 4 minutes, or until the chicken is cooked through and no pink remains. Whisk together the *Oyster Sauce* ingredients. Add the *Oyster Sauce* and cook until thickened, about 1 minute.

Sesame-Grilled Portabello Mushrooms | *serves 4*

3 Tbs.	rice vinegar
2 Tbs.	low-sodium soy sauce
1 tsp.	toasted sesame oil
1 Tbs.	fresh cilantro, minced
1 clove	garlic, minced
4 large	Portobello mushrooms, stems discarded and caps cleaned

In a small bowl, whisk together the rice vinegar, soy sauce, sesame oil, cilantro, and garlic. Place the mushroom caps in a self-sealing plastic bag and pour the mixture over them. Marinate for 20 minutes.

Place the Grilling Plate on the grill and preheat to high. Coat with nonfat cooking spray. Remove the mushrooms and place on the heated grill. Close the lid and grill for 5 to 6 minutes, or until the mushrooms have softened and are tender throughout.

CALORIES:
30

TOTAL FAT:
1g

SATURATED FAT:
<1g

% CAL FROM FAT:
41

CARBOHYDRATES:
3g

PROTEIN:
1g

CHOLESTEROL:
0mg

SODIUM:
254mg

Classic Korean BBQ | *serves 4*

1 lb.	lean beef sirloin, thinly sliced
3 Tbs.	sugar
2 Tbs.	toasted sesame oil
1 Tbs.	sesame seeds
½ cup	low-sodium soy sauce
5	green onions, thinly sliced
1 tsp.	freshly ground black pepper
½ tsp.	crushed red pepper flakes
	steamed white rice for 4, kept warm

In a self-sealing plastic bag, place all of the ingredients except the rice, combining well. Refrigerate for at least 6 hours or up to 8 hours.

Place the Grilling Plate on the grill and preheat to high. Coat with nonfat cooking spray. Remove the beef from the marinade and place on the grill. Close the lid and grill for 8 to 10 minutes, or until the beef is almost blackened. Serve over steamed white rice.

CALORIES:
321

TOTAL FAT:
7g

SATURATED FAT:
2g

% CAL FROM FAT:
19

CARBOHYDRATES:
34g

PROTEIN:
29g

CHOLESTEROL:
69mg

SODIUM:
1085mg

Thai Shrimp & Papaya Salad | *serves 4*

12 large	raw shrimp, deveined and shelled
1 tsp.	toasted sesame oil
¼ tsp.	Asian red chile paste
1½ cups	fresh papaya, cubed
6 cups	watercress or other baby field greens, cleaned
½ cup	whole cilantro leaves
1 small	red onion, peeled and sliced into rings
2 Tbs.	fresh lime juice
3 Tbs.	extra-virgin olive oil
1 tsp.	honey
¼ tsp.	salt
¼ tsp.	freshly ground black pepper

In a medium bowl, combine the shrimp, sesame oil, and red chile paste until the shrimp are well-coated. Set aside.

Place the papaya, watercress or field greens, cilantro leaves, and red onion in a large bowl. In a small bowl, whisk together the lime juice, olive oil, honey, salt, and pepper to form a vinaigrette.

Place the Grilling Plate on the grill and preheat to high. Coat with nonfat cooking spray. Place the shrimp on the grill and close the lid, grilling for about 3 minutes, or until the shrimp turn pink. Place the grilled shrimp on the salad and dress with the vinaigrette.

Tonkatsu Sauce (Japanese Dipping Sauce) | *serves 4*

½ cup	low-calorie ketchup
1 Tbs.	Worcestershire sauce
¼ tsp.	Dijon mustard
1 tsp.	low-sodium soy sauce

Whisk all ingredients together to combine.

Tamagoyaki | *makes 2 servings*

This rolled omelet is often served as a breakfast dish in Japan.

4 x-large	eggs, beaten, or egg substitute equivalent
3 Tbs.	water
2 tsp.	sugar
2 tsp.	low-sodium soy sauce
4	green onions, finely sliced
2 tsp.	vegetable oil

Place the Sauté Plate on the grill and preheat to medium-high. In a medium bowl, combine the eggs, water, sugar, soy sauce and onions. Beat well to blend. Drizzle a little oil in the Sauté Plate and pour a spoonful of the egg mixture into the plate. Use a knife to quickly spread the egg mixture over the surface. After one minute, roll the cooked egg and move it to the edge of the plate. Oil the Sauté Plate again and pour another spoonful of the egg mixture on the plate near and under the rolled egg. Cook for 1 minute and roll the egg again so that the rolled omelet becomes thicker.

Repeat this process until egg mixture has been used up. Remove the rolled omelet from the grill and place on a cutting board. Slice widthwise into 1-inch slices. Serve hot or cold.

CALORIES:
224

TOTAL FAT:
13g

SATURATED FAT:
4g

% CAL FROM FAT:
53

CARBOHYDRATES:
9g

PROTEIN:
17g

CHOLESTEROL:
553mg

SODIUM:
337mg

Grilled Miso Chicken | *serves 4*

2 Tbs.	miso paste
1 tsp.	toasted sesame oil
2 Tbs.	hot water
2 Tbs.	honey
4	boneless, skinless chicken breasts

In a small bowl, whisk together the miso paste, sesame oil, hot water, and honey. Place the chicken breasts in a self-sealing plastic bag and add the miso sauce, coating each piece of chicken thoroughly. Refrigerate for at least 1 hour or up to 8 hours.

Place the Grilling Plate on the grill and preheat to medium-high. Coat with nonfat cooking spray. Place the chicken on the grill and close the lid, grilling for 7 to 9 minutes, or until the chicken is cooked through and no pink remains.

CALORIES:
136

TOTAL FAT:
3g

SATURATED FAT:
<1g

% CAL FROM FAT:
17

CARBOHYDRATES:
10g

PROTEIN:
17g

CHOLESTEROL:
41mg

SODIUM:
360mg

Grilled Curry Chicken with Cucumber Mint Raita | *serves 4*

CALORIES:
172

TOTAL FAT:
5g

SATURATED FAT:
<1g

% CAL FROM FAT:
28

CARBOHYDRATES:
11g

PROTEIN:
20g

CHOLESTEROL:
45mg

SODIUM:
234mg

1 Tbs.	extra-virgin olive oil
2 tsp.	garam masala
2 tsp.	curry powder
1 tsp.	onion powder
1 tsp.	ground paprika
1 tsp.	ground cumin
½ tsp.	ground ginger
1 clove	garlic, minced
½ Tbs.	brown sugar, packed
4	boneless, skinless chicken breasts

Cucumber Mint Raita

1 cup	plain lowfat yogurt
¾ cup	cucumber, peeled and grated
2 Tbs.	fresh mint leaves, minced
2 Tbs.	fresh lemon juice
¼ tsp.	freshly ground black pepper
¼ tsp.	salt

Whisk together the olive oil, garam masala, curry, onion powder, paprika, cumin, ginger, garlic, and brown sugar. Place the chicken breasts in a self-sealing plastic bag and add the spice mixture, coating each piece thoroughly. Refrigerate for at least 1 hour or up to 8 hours.

Place the Grilling Plate on the grill and preheat to medium-high. Coat with nonfat cooking spray. Place the chicken on the grill and close the lid, grilling for 7 to 9 minutes, or until the chicken is cooked through and no pink remains. Meanwhile, combine the *Cucumber Mint Raita* ingredients in a small bowl. Serve the chicken with the raita on the side.

Filipino Pork Pancit | *serves 3*

CALORIES:
234

TOTAL FAT:
3g

SATURATED FAT:
<1g

% CAL FROM FAT:
13

CARBOHYDRATES:
39g

PROTEIN:
13g

CHOLESTEROL:
25mg

SODIUM:
612mg

3 oz.	dried rice noodles
1 tsp.	vegetable oil
¼ lb.	pork tenderloin, cut into bite-sized pieces
½ med.	yellow onion, peeled and finely diced
2 cloves	garlic, minced
½ small	head green cabbage, thinly sliced
2 med.	carrots, peeled and thinly sliced
3 Tbs.	low-sodium soy sauce

Place the Sauté Plate on the grill and preheat to medium-high. Place the rice noodles in a large bowl and cover with hot water. When soft, drain and set aside.

Heat the oil in the Sauté Plate and add the pork, onion, and garlic, cooking for 4 minutes. Add the cabbage, carrots, and soy sauce. Cook and stir for another 4 minutes, or until the pork is cooked through. Toss in the noodles and stir as the noodles warm.

Korean BBQ Sandwich | *serves 2*

½ lb.	*Classic Korean BBQ* (p. 27)
2	French rolls, cut in half lengthwise and widthwise
2 Tbs.	kimchi (found in the Asian section of your grocery store)
10 slices	pickled daikon radish (found in the Asian section of your grocery store)
1	Roma tomato, thinly sliced

Place the Grilling Plate on the grill and preheat to medium-high. Remove some of the white bread filling from the interior of the rolls to create a space for the sandwich filling. Layer the *Korean BBQ* beef, kimchi, daikon, and tomato slices in-between the roll slices. Place each filled roll half on the grill and close the lid. Grill for 3 minutes, or until the rolls are toasty and the filling is warm.

CALORIES:
289

TOTAL FAT:
5g

SATURATED FAT:
1g

% CAL FROM FAT:
16

CARBOHYDRATES:
41g

PROTEIN:
18g

CHOLESTEROL:
35mg

SODIUM:
1533mg

Bun Thit Nuong (Vietnamese Cool Noodle Salad) | *serves 4*

2 cups	green leaf lettuce, shredded
1 cup	fresh bean sprouts, rinsed
½ fresh	cucumber, peeled and julienned
½ large	carrot, peeled and julienned
2 Tbs.	mint leaves, roughly chopped
2 Tbs.	Thai basil leaves, roughly chopped
6 oz.	rice vermicelli (or angel hair pasta), cooked and rinsed with cold water
1 lb.	*Vietnamese Pork Skewers* (p. 32)
3 Tbs.	shallots (or substitute fried onion rings)
4 Tbs.	roasted peanuts, chopped
1 cup	*Nuoc Cham Dipping Sauce* (p. 32)

Toss together the lettuce, bean sprouts, cucumbers, carrot, mint, and basil. Divide the vegetables among 4 large bowls. Top each with one-fourth of the noodles. Remove the pork from the skewers and divide among the bowls, topping the noodles. Garnish each salad with the shallots, peanuts, and 4 tablespoons of the sauce. Toss just before serving.

CALORIES:
455

TOTAL FAT:
9g

SATURATED FAT:
2g

% CAL FROM FAT:
18

CARBOHYDRATES:
53g

PROTEIN:
35g

CHOLESTEROL:
83mg

SODIUM:
2568mg

Vietnamese Pork Skewers | *serves 4*

CALORIES:
263

TOTAL FAT:
6g

SATURATED FAT:
2g

% CAL FROM FAT:
21

CARBOHYDRATES:
13g

PROTEIN:
37g

CHOLESTEROL:
111mg

SODIUM:
1922mg

Lemongrass Marinade

2 stalks	lemongrass, finely minced
1 clove	garlic, finely minced
1 tsp.	sugar
1 Tbs.	fish sauce
1	red chili, finely diced
½ tsp.	ground black pepper

1½ lbs.	pork tenderloin, cut into long, thin strips
12	wooden skewers, soaked in water for 30 minutes

Nuoc Cham Dipping Sauce

2 cloves	garlic, minced
1 small	shallot, minced
1	jalapeño or Serrano pepper, seeded and minced
2 Tbs.	sugar
¼ cup	fish sauce
2 Tbs.	rice vinegar
2 Tbs.	fresh lime juice
1 large	carrot, finely shredded
3 Tbs.	warm water

In a self-sealing plastic bag, combine the *Lemongrass Marinade* ingredients and the pork. Mix until the pork is well-coated and refrigerate for at least 1 hour or up to 8 hours.

Place the Grilling Plate on the grill and preheat the grill to high. Coat with nonfat cooking spray. Remove the pork from the marinade and thread each piece onto a skewer. Place on the grill, close the lid and grill for 5-6 minutes, or until the pork is cooked through.

While the pork is grilling, whisk together the *Nuoc Cham Dipping Sauce* ingredients in a small bowl. Remove the skewers from the grill and serve with the dipping sauce. If desired, serve over a bed of rice vermicelli noodles.

Chapter ~ Three

G100™
LATIN AMERICAN FLAVORS!

Chili-Cumin Rubbed Pork Tenderloin | *serves 4*

1 tsp.	chili powder
1 tsp.	ground cumin
1 tsp.	dried oregano
1½ tsp.	garlic powder
½ tsp.	salt
½. tsp.	freshly ground black pepper
¼ tsp.	cayenne pepper
2 (¾ lbs. each)	pork tenderloins

In a small bowl, combine the spices. Rub the spices all over the pork tenderloins and place in a large, self-sealing plastic bag. Refrigerate for at least 3 hours or up to 8 hours.

Place the Grilling Plate on the grill and preheat to medium-high. Coat with nonfat cooking spray. Place the pork tenderloins on the grill, close the lid, and grill for 10 to 12 minutes, or until the pork is cooked through. The pork should be cooked to at least 160ºF on a meat thermometer. Slice before serving.

CALORIES:
385

TOTAL FAT:
11g

SATURATED FAT:
4g

% CAL FROM FAT:
27

CARBOHYDRATES:
2g

PROTEIN:
66g

CHOLESTEROL:
203mg

SODIUM:
455mg

Seared Steak Tacos | *serves 6*

CALORIES:
466

TOTAL FAT:
24g

SATURATED FAT:
8g

% CAL FROM FAT:
44

CARBOHYDRATES:
36g

PROTEIN:
30g

CHOLESTEROL:
68mg

SODIUM:
731mg

4 cloves	garlic, minced
1 tsp.	chili powder
1 tsp.	dried oregano
	juice of 2 limes, divided
½ tsp.	freshly ground black pepper
1 tsp.	salt, divided
1½ lbs.	lean flank steak
1 med.	tomato, finely chopped
2 ripe	avocados, diced
¼ red	onion, diced
½	jalapeño pepper, seeded and finely diced
1½ Tbs.	fresh cilantro, minced
12	6-inch corn tortillas
½ cup	queso fresco cheese, crumbled (you may use shredded Monterey Jack cheese)

Combine the garlic, chili powder, oregano, the juice of one lime, black pepper and ½ teaspoon salt in a small bowl. Pat the mixture all over the flank steak and place in a self-sealing plastic bag. Refrigerate for at least 3 hours or up to 8 hours.

Place the Grilling Plate on the grill and preheat to medium-high. Coat with nonfat cooking spray. Place the beef on the grill, close the lid, and grill for 6 to 8 minutes, or until the steak is cooked to your choice. Meanwhile, combine the tomato, avocados, onion, pepper, cilantro, the juice of one lime, and ½ teaspoon of salt in a medium bowl. Remove the steak from the grill and let rest for 5 minutes. Slice thinly against the grain. Meanwhile, place the corn tortillas on the grill, overlapping to fit, and grill on medium-high heat for 2 to 3 minutes, or until warm. To make the tacos, top each corn tortilla with a little sliced steak, tomato mixture, and cheese.

Chicken & Bean Tortas | *serves 4*

3	boneless, skinless chicken breasts
2 Tbs.	fresh lime juice
1 tsp.	chili powder
1 clove	garlic, minced
4	French bread rolls (or bolillos)
15 oz.	can lowfat refried beans
½ cup	lowfat Monterey Jack cheese, shredded (or crumbled queso anejo)
2 cups	iceberg lettuce, shredded
½ cup	red radishes, thinly sliced

In a self-sealing plastic bag, combine the chicken breasts, lime juice, chili powder, and garlic. Refrigerate for 30 minutes. Place the Grilling Plate on the grill and preheat to medium-high. Coat with nonfat cooking spray. Place the chicken on the grill, close the lid, and grill for 7 to 9 minutes, or until chicken is cooked through and no pink remains. Remove the chicken and cut into diagonal slices when cool.

Open the bread rolls and spread each half with refried beans. Sprinkle with cheese and place the chicken slices inside. Close the rolls and place on the grill on medium-high heat. Close the lid and grill for 3 minutes, or until the cheese melts and the rolls are crusty. Remove from the grill, and add the lettuce and radishes to each sandwich.

CALORIES:
317

TOTAL FAT:
8g

SATURATED FAT:
3g

% CAL FROM FAT:
21

CARBOHYDRATES:
40g

PROTEIN:
26g

CHOLESTEROL:
40mg

SODIUM:
876mg

Chili-Rubbed Prawns | *serves 4*

½ tsp.	ground black pepper
1 tsp.	cayenne pepper
1 tsp.	chili powder
1 tsp.	ground cumin
1 tsp.	brown sugar, packed
½ tsp.	ground oregano
2 tsp.	ground paprika
1 tsp.	salt
1½ lbs.	large shrimp, peeled and deveined

In a small bowl, combine the spices thoroughly. Rub the spices all over the shrimp and place in a large, self-sealing plastic bag. Refrigerate for at least 1 to 3 hours.

Place the Grilling Plate on the grill and preheat to high. Coat with nonfat cooking spray. Place the shrimp on the grill in a single layer, close the lid, and grill for 3 to 4 minutes, or until the shrimp are pink and cooked through.

CALORIES:
196

TOTAL FAT:
3g

SATURATED FAT:
<1g

% CAL FROM FAT:
16

CARBOHYDRATES:
4g

PROTEIN:
35g

CHOLESTEROL:
259mg

SODIUM:
842mg

Roasted Chile Rellenos | *serves 2*

CALORIES:
421

TOTAL FAT:
25g

SATURATED FAT:
16g

% CAL FROM FAT:
51

CARBOHYDRATES:
28g

PROTEIN:
27g

CHOLESTEROL:
76mg

SODIUM:
546mg

4 large	Anaheim chile peppers
3 oz.	lowfat Monterey Jack cheese, shredded
3 oz.	goat cheese, semi-soft, crumbled
¼ cup	lowfat sour cream
¼ cup	fresh pico de gallo (or use fresh salsa)

Cut open one side of each pepper and remove the core and seeds. Place the Grilling Plate on the grill and preheat to high. Coat with nonfat cooking spray. Place the peppers on the grill, close the lid, and grill for 10 to 15 minutes, or until softened and blackened. Place the peppers in a paper bag, seal tightly, and let sit for 10 minutes to steam. Remove and carefully peel the outer skins off each pepper.

Stuff one-half of each pepper with the cheeses and wrap to form a whole pepper again. Place on the grill. Reduce the heat to medium. Grill for 2 to 3 minutes, or until the cheese has melted. Serve each pepper with a dollop of sour cream and pico de gallo.

Chipotle-Citrus Flank Steak | *serves 4*

CALORIES:
289

TOTAL FAT:
13g

SATURATED FAT:
5g

% CAL FROM FAT:
41

CARBOHYDRATES:
6g

PROTEIN:
35g

CHOLESTEROL:
85mg

SODIUM:
844mg

4 cloves	garlic, minced
2 canned	chipotle chiles, finely chopped
1 tsp.	dried oregano
	juice of 1 lime
	juice of 1 orange
½ tsp.	salt
½ tsp.	freshly ground black pepper
1½ lbs.	lean flank steak

Place garlic, chiles, oregano, lime juice, orange juice, salt and pepper in a blender and purée until smooth. Place in a self-sealing plastic bag with the flank steak and refrigerate at least 3 hours or up to 8 hours.

Place the Grilling Plate on the grill and preheat to medium-high. Coat with nonfat cooking spray. Place the marinated beef on the grill, close the lid, and grill for 6 to 8 minutes, or until the steak is cooked to your choice. Slice the cooked beef thinly against the grain of the beef.

Seared Fish Fillets in Escabeche Sauce | *serves 2*

1 Tbs.	extra-virgin olive oil
2 6 oz.	halibut steaks, bone removed, lightly seasoned with salt & pepper

Escabeche Sauce

1 large	white onion, thinly sliced
2 med.	carrots, peeled and grated or julienned
3 Tbs.	white vinegar
1	bay leaf, crumbled
1 clove	garlic, minced
½ tsp.	salt
½ tsp.	freshly ground black pepper
1 pinch	crushed red pepper flakes

Place the Sauté Plate on the grill and preheat to medium-high. Add the olive oil. When heated, add the halibut steaks, close the lid, and sauté for 7 minutes, or until the fish is cooked through and flakes easily. Remove the fish and keep warm.

Place the remaining ingredients in the Sauté Plate and use a plastic spoon to stir and combine until well-mixed. Close the lid and cook for 5 minutes, or until the onion and carrots are softened, yet slightly crisp. Spoon the *Escabeche Sauce* over the halibut steaks before serving.

CALORIES:
314

TOTAL FAT:
11g

SATURATED FAT:
<1g

% CAL FROM FAT:
33

CARBOHYDRATES:
14g

PROTEIN:
37g

CHOLESTEROL:
55mg

SODIUM:
893mg

Camarones al Mojo de Ajo (Shrimp with Garlic) | *serves 4*

1½ lbs.	large shrimp, cleaned, peeled, and deveined
1 Tbs.	extra-virgin olive oil
½ tsp.	salt
½ tsp.	freshly ground black pepper
1 tsp.	ground cumin
½	chipotle pepper, minced
7 cloves	garlic, minced
2 Tbs.	margarine or lowfat butter-flavored spread
2 Tbs.	fresh lime juice
1 Tbs.	fresh cilantro, minced

Place the Sauté Plate on the grill and preheat to medium-high. Coat with nonfat cooking spray. Combine the shrimp, oil, salt, pepper, cumin, and pepper in a medium bowl and blend until well-mixed. Add the shrimp to the Sauté Plate and cook for about 3 minutes, or until the shrimp is pink. Remove from the grill and set aside. Drain the liquid from the Sauté Plate.

Place the garlic and margarine in the Sauté Plate and cook for 3 minutes, or until the garlic are golden and the butter is melted. Add the cooked shrimp, lime juice, and cilantro and toss lightly to combine. Cook for 1 minute.

CALORIES:
239

TOTAL FAT:
8g

SATURATED FAT:
1g

% CAL FROM FAT:
31

CARBOHYDRATES:
5g

PROTEIN:
35g

CHOLESTEROL:
259mg

SODIUM:
600mg

Roasted Vegetable Quesadillas | *serves 4*

CALORIES:
396

TOTAL FAT:
10g

SATURATED FAT:
6g

% CAL FROM FAT:
23

CARBOHYDRATES:
61g

PROTEIN:
17g

CHOLESTEROL:
32mg

SODIUM:
1229mg

1 tsp.	extra-virgin olive oil
1 tsp.	dried oregano
2 cloves	garlic, minced
½ tsp.	salt
1 med.	zucchini, cut into ½-inch slices
1 large	Portobello mushroom, cut into strips
1 large	red onion, peeled and cut into rings
1 red	bell pepper, seeded and thinly sliced
4 oz.	Gouda cheese, grated
8 large	lowfat flour tortillas

Place the Grilling Plate on the grill and preheat to medium-high. Coat with nonfat cooking spray. In a large bowl, combine the oil, oregano, garlic, salt, zucchini, mushrooms, onion, and red bell pepper, mixing until the vegetables are well-coated with seasoning. Place the vegetables on the grill, close the lid and grill for 5 minutes, or until the vegetables are tender. Remove and keep warm.

Place a large flour tortilla on the Grilling Plate and top with one-fourth of the grilled vegetables and cheese. Top with another flour tortilla and close the lid. Grill for 2 minutes on high heat until the cheese is melted. Repeat with the remaining tortillas and fillings.

Pupusas con Queso (El Salvadoran Tortillas with Cheese) | *makes about 10 pupusas*

CALORIES:
151

TOTAL FAT:
7g

SATURATED FAT:
2g

% CAL FROM FAT:
40

CARBOHYDRATES:
18g

PROTEIN:
5g

CHOLESTEROL:
6mg

SODIUM:
61mg

2 cups	masa harina flour (available in the specialty food aisle of the grocery store)
1 cup	water (approximately)
1 cup	part-skim mozzarella cheese, shredded
2 Tbs.	canola oil

In a medium bowl, stir enough water into the masa harina flour until a firm dough is formed that can be shaped into a ball. Add more water, if necessary. Divide the dough into 10 pieces. Roll each into a ball and flatten between the palms of your hands so that they are each about ½-inch thick. Using your thumb, create a slight depression in the center of the flattened dough and fill with cheese. Enclose the dough firmly around the cheese. Flatten again, keeping the cheese filling inside.

Meanwhile, place the Sauté Plate on the grill and preheat to medium. Brush each pupusa with a little canola oil and place on the grill, cooking in batches if needed. Close the lid and cook for 5 minutes, or until each pupusa is heated through and golden.

Argentinean Steaks with Chimichurri Sauce | *serves 4*

Chimichurri Sauce

8 cloves	garlic, coarsely chopped
1	jalapeño pepper, coarsely chopped
1 cup	fresh flat leaf parsley leaves
¼ cup	red wine vinegar
½ cup	extra-virgin olive oil
1 tsp.	dried oregano
½ tsp.	salt
4 6 oz.	boneless, New York strip steaks, fat removed

In a food processor or blender, combine the garlic, jalapeño pepper, parsley, vinegar, oil, oregano, and salt until smooth. Place the steaks in a large self-sealing plastic bag, with half of the blended *Chimichurri Sauce*. Reserve the other half of the sauce to serve with the cooked steaks. Refrigerate the steaks for at least 1 hour or up to 8 hours.

Place the Grilling Plate on the grill and preheat to medium-high. Coat with nonfat cooking spray. Place the steaks on the grill, close the lid, and grill for 5 to 6 minutes, or until the steaks are cooked to your preference. Remove the steaks from the grill and let rest for at least 5 minutes. Serve with the remaining half of the *Chimichurri Sauce*.

CALORIES:
304

TOTAL FAT:
15g

SATURATED FAT:
3g

% CAL FROM FAT:
45

CARBOHYDRATES:
3g

PROTEIN:
38g

CHOLESTEROL:
100mg

SODIUM:
493mg

Roasted Tomato Salsa | *serves 6*

6	Roma tomatoes, cut in half
½ large	yellow onion, cut into rings
1 tsp.	extra-virgin olive oil
3 cloves	garlic, coarsely chopped
½	jalapeño pepper, stemmed, seeded, and finely diced
2 Tbs.	fresh cilantro, minced
	juice of 1 lime
½ tsp.	salt
½ tsp.	ground cumin

Place the Grilling Plate on the grill and preheat to high. Coat with nonfat cooking spray. In a large bowl, combine the tomatoes, onion, and olive oil. Place the vegetables on the grill and close the lid, cooking for 8 minutes. Remove from the grill and place in a food processor or blender with the remaining ingredients. Purée until smooth.

CALORIES:
43

TOTAL FAT:
3g

SATURATED FAT:
<1g

% CAL FROM FAT:
49

CARBOHYDRATES:
5g

PROTEIN:
<1g

CHOLESTEROL:
0mg

SODIUM:
231mg

Jalapeño & Cheese Turkey Burgers | *serves 4*

CALORIES: 447

TOTAL FAT: 22g

SATURATED FAT: 7g

% CAL FROM FAT: 44

CARBOHYDRATES: 31g

PROTEIN: 32g

CHOLESTEROL: 110mg

SODIUM: 1105mg

1 lb.	ground turkey
1 cup	plum tomatoes, seeded and chopped
¼ cup	fresh cilantro, minced
1 Tbs.	chili powder
½	seeded jalapeño pepper, minced
½ tsp.	salt
½ tsp.	dried oregano
½ tsp.	ground cumin
¼ tsp.	freshly ground black pepper
4 slices	reduced-fat pepper Jack cheese
1 cup	prepared guacamole
4	whole grain hamburger buns
4 slices	ripe tomato
4 leaves	dark green lettuce

In a large bowl, mix the together the turkey, tomato, cilantro, chili powder, jalapeño pepper, salt, oregano, cumin, and black pepper until just combined. Divide the mixture into 4 equal portions and shape into ½-inch-thick patties.

Place the Grilling Plate on the grill and preheat to medium-high. Coat with nonfat cooking spray. Place the patties on the grill, close the lid, and grill for 6 to 8 minutes, or until the patties are cooked through and no pink remains. In the last minute of cooking, open the grill and place the cheese slices on top of the patties.

Spread ¼ cup of the guacamole on the top and bottom halves of each hamburger bun and add the turkey patties, tomato slices, and lettuce.

Huevos Ahogados | *serves 4*

CALORIES: 113

TOTAL FAT: 5g

SATURATED FAT: 2g

% CAL FROM FAT: 40

CARBOHYDRATES: 10g

PROTEIN: 7g

CHOLESTEROL: 213mg

SODIUM: 262mg

Literally meaning "drowned eggs," these tasty eggs are poached in a flavorful tomato sauce and are a delicious alternative to the typical "Huevos Rancheros."

¼ med.	yellow onion
2 cloves	garlic, minced
14.5 oz.	can stewed tomatoes
2 tsp.	chili powder
4 large	eggs

Place the Sauté Plate on the grill and preheat to medium-high. In a blender or food processor, purée the onion, garlic, tomatoes, and chili powder until smooth.

Pour half of the tomato sauce into the Sauté Plate and add the eggs. Close the lid and cook for 6 to 7 minutes, or until the eggs are soft-cooked . Meanwhile, heat the remaining tomato sauce in the microwave or on the stovetop until hot. Remove the eggs from the grill and top with the heated, remaining tomato sauce. Serve with refried beans and tortillas on the side.

Grilled Swordfish Tacos with Roasted Mango Salsa | *serves 4*

2 6 oz.	swordfish steaks (or other firm, white fish)
¼ tsp.	salt
½ tsp.	chili powder
½ cup	reduced-fat mayonnaise
½ cup	nonfat sour cream
1 4 oz.	can diced green chilies
1 cup	*Roasted Mango Salsa*
¼ small	head of cabbage, shredded (or iceberg lettuce)
8 6-inch	corn tortillas, warmed

Place the Grilling Plate on the grill and preheat to medium-high. Coat with nonstick cooking spray. Season the swordfish with the salt and chili powder. Place on the Grill Plate and close the lid. Grill for 8 to 10 minutes, or until the fish flakes easily. Meanwhile, make the white sauce by placing the mayonnaise, sour cream, and chilies in a blender or food processor and pulse until well-combined.

Remove the swordfish from the grill and flake the steaks, removing any bone or cartilage. To serve, place one-eighth of the fish, shredded cabbage, white sauce, and salsa in the middle of each tortilla, roll up, and enjoy.

CALORIES:
373

TOTAL FAT:
10g

SATURATED FAT:
2g

% CAL FROM FAT:
24

CARBOHYDRATES:
49g

PROTEIN:
23g

CHOLESTEROL:
38mg

SODIUM:
781mg

Roasted Mango Salsa | *makes about 2 1/2 cups (serves 5)*

1 large	ripe mango, peeled, pitted and cut lengthwise into ½-inch slices
½ med.	red onion, finely chopped
1	jalapeño pepper, finely minced
1 small	cucumber, peeled and diced
1 ripe	avocado, finely chopped
3 Tbs.	fresh cilantro leaves, finely chopped
3 Tbs.	fresh lime juice
¼ tsp.	salt

Place the Grilling Plate on the grill and preheat to high. Coat with nonstick cooking spray. Place the mango slices on the grill, close the lid, and grill for 3 minutes. Remove from the grill and cool. Dice the grilled mango and combine with the remaining ingredients in a medium bowl.

CALORIES:
101

TOTAL FAT:
6g

SATURATED FAT:
<1g

% CAL FROM FAT:
50

CARBOHYDRATES:
13g

PROTEIN:
1g

CHOLESTEROL:
0mg

SODIUM:
196mg

Blackened Chicken & Avocado Tostadas | *serves 8*

CALORIES:
171

TOTAL FAT:
11g

SATURATED FAT:
2g

% CAL FROM FAT:
50

CARBOHYDRATES:
14g

PROTEIN:
10g

CHOLESTEROL:
38mg

SODIUM:
258mg

3	boneless, skinless chicken breasts
1 Tbs.	ground paprika
1 tsp.	ground cumin
1 tsp.	dried oregano
1 tsp.	garlic powder
¼ tsp.	cayenne pepper
1 ripe	avocado, pitted and peeled, cut into 8 slices
1 Tbs.	fresh lime juice
8	tostada shells
2 cups	romaine lettuce, shredded
1 cup	prepared salsa
¼ cup	lowfat sour cream
2.25 oz.	can black sliced olives, drained

In a self-sealing plastic bag, combine the chicken breasts, paprika, cumin, oregano, garlic powder, and cayenne pepper. Refrigerate for at least 1 hour or overnight.

Place the Grilling Plate on the grill and preheat to high. Coat with nonstick cooking spray. In a small bowl, combine the avocado slices and lime juice until well-coated. Place the avocado slices on the grill, close the lid, and grill for 2 minutes. Remove from the grill and set aside.

Place the chicken on the grill, close the lid, and cook for 7 to 9 minutes, or until the chicken is cooked through and no pink remains. Cool and slice into ¼-inch thick slices. To assemble the tostadas, top each tostada shell with chicken, avocado, lettuce, salsa, sour cream, and sliced olives.

Pork Chops Adobo | *serves 4*

Adobo Sauce

2	ancho chilies, stemmed, seeded, and torn into large pieces
1 tsp.	vegetable oil
1 clove	garlic, chopped
½ small	yellow onion, roughly chopped
1 cup	low-sodium chicken broth
¼ tsp.	dried oregano leaves
¼ tsp.	freshly ground black pepper
pinch	ground cumin
1 Tbs.	cider vinegar
½ tsp.	dark brown sugar, packed
¼ tsp.	salt
4 6 oz.	bone-in center-cut pork chops, trimmed of fat
1 Tbs.	fresh orange juice
1 Tbs.	fresh lime juice

In a skillet, heat the chilie pieces over medium heat, for a quick 30 seconds. Remove the chilies from the pan and add the oil, garlic, and onion to the pan, and cook for 5 minutes, or until browned. In a small saucepan on medium heat, combine the heated chilie pieces, garlic, onion, chicken broth, oregano, pepper, cumin, 1 Tbs. cider vinegar, brown sugar and salt. Bring to a boil, reduce to a simmer, and simmer for 5 minutes. Pour the mixture into a blender and blend until smooth. Let cool.

Place the pork chops and cooled *Adobo Sauce* into a self-sealing plastic bag and marinate, refrigerated, for at least 8 hours or overnight.

Place the Grilling Plate on the grill and preheat to medium-high. Coat with nonfat cooking spray. Place the pork chops on the grill and close the lid. Cook for 5 to 6 minutes, or until the pork is cooked through. In the last minute of cooking, drizzle with the orange and lime juices.

CALORIES:
286

TOTAL FAT:
10g

SATURATED FAT:
3g

% CAL FROM FAT:
34

CARBOHYDRATES:
8g

PROTEIN:
39g

CHOLESTEROL:
107mg

SODIUM:
262mg

Grilled Chicken, Jicama & Papaya Salad with Lime Vinaigrette | *serves 6*

3	boneless, skinless chicken breasts
2 Tbs.	fresh lime juice
1 tsp.	chili powder
1 clove	garlic, minced
4 cups	lettuce, shredded
2 cups	jicama, julienned
1 cup	fresh papaya, cubed
1 cup	carrot, shredded
3	green onions, finely sliced
2 Tbs.	fresh cilantro, minced

Lime Vinaigrette

¼ cup	fresh lime juice
2½ Tbs.	extra-virgin olive oil
1 Tbs.	honey
¼ tsp.	salt
¼ tsp.	freshly ground black pepper

In a self-sealing plastic bag, combine the chicken, lime juice, chili powder, and garlic. Refrigerate for 30 minutes.

Place the Grilling Plate on the grill and preheat to medium-high. Coat with nonfat cooking spray. Place the chicken on the grill, close the lid and grill for 7 to 9 minutes, or until the chicken is cooked through and no pink remains. Remove the chicken and cut into diagonal slices when cool. In a large bowl, combine the lettuce, jicama, papaya, carrot, onions, and cilantro. In a small bowl, whisk together the *Lime Vinaigrette* ingredients and pour over the salad. Top each salad serving with the chicken.

CALORIES: 147
TOTAL FAT: 7g
SATURATED FAT: <1g
% CAL FROM FAT: 39
CARBOHYDRATES: 14g
PROTEIN: 10g
CHOLESTEROL: 21mg
SODIUM: 139mg

Blackened Corn with Chili-Cilantro Glaze | *serves 4*

2 Tbs.	cilantro, finely chopped
1 tsp.	chili powder
¼ tsp.	salt
2 Tbs.	lowfat butter-flavored spread, melted
4 small	ears of corn, husks and silk removed
1 Tbs.	Parmesan cheese, freshly grated

Place the Grilling Plate on the grill and preheat to high. In a small bowl, whisk together the cilantro, chili powder, salt, and melted butter. Using a pastry brush, brush the mixture all over the corn. Place the corn on the grill and close the lid. Grill for 3 minutes. Open the lid and rotate the corn one-quarter turn. Grill for an additional 3 minutes, with the lid closed. Garnish the corn with the Parmesan cheese just before serving.

CALORIES: 85
TOTAL FAT: 3g
SATURATED FAT: 1g
% CAL FROM FAT: 28
CARBOHYDRATES: 14g
PROTEIN: 3g
CHOLESTEROL: >1mg
SODIUM: 246mg

Cuban Fritas | *serves 4*

These Cuban hamburgers are traditionally served as "sliders" – small hamburgers, about half the size of a normal burger. You can achieve this by using a round biscuit cutter to cut hamburger buns to a smaller size and making 8 patties instead of 4.

¼ cup	lowfat milk
½ cup	bread crumbs
1 lb.	lean ground beef
1	egg (or equivalent egg substitute)
¼ med.	white onion, finely chopped
½ tsp.	ground paprika
2 tsp.	Thousand Island dressing
½ tsp.	salt
½ tsp.	freshly ground black pepper
4	hamburger buns

Place the milk and bread crumbs in a large mixing bowl and let soak for 1 minute. Add the remaining ingredients except the buns and mix until just combined. Divide the mixture into 4 equal portions and shape into ½-inch thick patties. Cover in plastic wrap and refrigerate for 1 hour to allow flavors to meld.

Place the Grilling Plate on the grill and preheat to medium-high. Coat with nonfat cooking spray. Place the patties on the grill, close the lid, and grill for 5 minutes or until cooked to your choice. Place the patties on the hamburger buns and serve with accompaniments or garnishes.

CALORIES:
318

TOTAL FAT:
8g

SATURATED FAT:
5g

% CAL FROM FAT:
25

CARBOHYDRATES:
26g

PROTEIN:
30g

CHOLESTEROL:
123mg

SODIUM:
653mg

Cuban Sandwich | *serves 1*

1	French sandwich roll
1 tsp.	margarine or lowfat butter-flavored spread
1 tsp.	prepared Dijon mustard
1 oz.	roasted pork, thinly sliced
1 oz.	smoked ham, thinly sliced
1 slice	lowfat Swiss cheese
2 slices	dill or bread & butter pickles

Place the Grilling Plate on the grill and preheat to medium-high. Coat with nonfat cooking spray. Lightly butter the exterior of the roll with margarine. Fill the roll with the remaining ingredients. Place the sandwich on the grill, close the lid, and grill for 3 minutes, or until the cheese melts and the bread is toasted. Garnish with the pickles before serving.

CALORIES:
293

TOTAL FAT:
10g

SATURATED FAT:
4g

% CAL FROM FAT:
33

CARBOHYDRATES:
22g

PROTEIN:
25g

CHOLESTEROL:
50mg

SODIUM:
946mg

Jamaican Jerk Chicken | *serves 4*

CALORIES:
175

TOTAL FAT:
5g

SATURATED FAT:
<1g

% CAL FROM FAT:
26

CARBOHYDRATES:
11g

PROTEIN:
21g

CHOLESTEROL:
41mg

SODIUM:
1443mg

1	habañero pepper
1 med.	onion, peeled and chopped
2	green onions, chopped
3 cloves	garlic, chopped
1 Tbs.	five-spice powder
1 Tbs.	freshly ground black pepper
1 tsp.	dried thyme
½ tsp.	salt
1 tsp.	ground nutmeg
½ cup	low-sodium soy sauce
1 Tbs.	extra-virgin olive oil
1 Tbs.	fresh lime juice
4	boneless, skinless chicken breasts

Wearing gloves, carefully seed and chop the pepper. (The oil can burn your skin or eyes on contact.) Place the pepper in a blender or food processor and add the remaining ingredients except the chicken. Process until smooth. Place the marinade with the chicken in a self-sealing plastic bag and refrigerate for at least 4 hours or up to 8 hours.

Place the Grilling Plate on the grill and preheat to high. Coat with nonfat cooking spray. Remove the chicken from the marinade and place on the grill. Close the lid and grill for 7 to 9 minutes, or until no pink remains and the chicken is cooked through.

Costillitas (Cuban Ribs) | *serves 4*

CALORIES:
273

TOTAL FAT:
11g

SATURATED FAT:
4g

% CAL FROM FAT:
38

CARBOHYDRATES:
4g

PROTEIN:
37g

CHOLESTEROL:
94mg

SODIUM:
659mg

3 cloves	garlic, minced
	juice of 1 large lemon
¼ tsp.	ground oregano
3 Tbs.	fresh orange juice
2 Tbs.	fresh lime juice
1 tsp.	salt
1½ lbs.	country style boneless pork ribs

Combine the garlic, lemon juice, oregano, orange juice, lime juice, and salt in a small bowl. Reserve 3 tablespoons of the sauce to be used later. Place the pork ribs and citrus marinade in a self-sealing plastic bag and refrigerate for at least 3 hours or up to 8 hours.

Place the Grilling Plate on the grill and preheat to medium-high. Coat with nonfat cooking spray. Place the ribs on the Grilling Plate and close the lid. Grill for 8 to 10 minutes or until cooked through. The internal temperature of the pork should reach at least 160ºF on a meat thermometer when done. In the last minute of cooking, baste with the reserved citrus marinade.

Fried Plantains | *serves 2*

2 ripe	yellow plantains (skins should be partially black)
2 tsp.	vegetable oil, divided
2 tsp.	powdered sugar

Cut the plantains diagonally, into ¼-inch slices. Place the Sauté Plate on the grill and preheat to medium-high. Drizzle 1 teaspoon of the oil on the grill and add half of the plantain slices. Fry until golden, about 3 minutes per side. Remove from the grill and dust with sugar. Repeat with the remaining plaintains. Serve over ice cream or frozen yogurt.

CALORIES:
269

TOTAL FAT:
5g

SATURATED FAT:
<1g

% CAL FROM FAT:
16

CARBOHYDRATES:
60g

PROTEIN:
2g

CHOLESTEROL:
0mg

SODIUM:
7mg

Torrejas (Cuban French Toast) | *serves 4*

4	eggs, beaten (or equivalent egg substitute)
1 cup	evaporated milk
½ cup	granulated white sugar
½ tsp.	pure vanilla extract
½ tsp.	ground cinnamon
8 slices	of day-old white bread
2 tsp.	vegetable oil, divided

Place the Sauté Plate on the grill and preheat to medium-high. Coat with nonfat cooking spray. In a medium bowl, combine the eggs, milk, sugar, vanilla, and cinnamon. Drizzle 1 teaspoon of oil on the grill. Dip four pieces of bread into the egg mixture and, when soaked, place on the Sauté Plate. Cook until golden, about 3 minutes per side. Repeat with the remaining slices. Serve as breakfast or as a dessert, with fresh fruit on top.

CALORIES:
414

TOTAL FAT:
14g

SATURATED FAT:
5g

% CAL FROM FAT:
29

CARBOHYDRATES:
60g

PROTEIN:
15g

CHOLESTEROL:
231mg

SODIUM:
430mg

Grilled Pineapple with Ginger-Lime Glaze | *serves 6*

CALORIES:
100

TOTAL FAT:
<1g

SATURATED FAT:
<1g

% CAL FROM FAT:
3

CARBOHYDRATES:
26g

PROTEIN:
<1g

CHOLESTEROL:
0mg

SODIUM:
<1mg

1 Tbs.	fresh ginger, grated
6 Tbs.	honey
4 Tbs.	water
1 tsp.	lime zest
1 Tbs.	fresh lime juice
1 med.	pineapple, cored, peeled and cut into 1-inch thick slices

In a small saucepan, combine the ginger, honey, water, lime zest, and lime juice. Bring to a boil and reduce to a simmer. Cook and stir for 2 minutes. Remove from the grill and set aside.

Place the Grilling Plate on the grill and preheat to high. Coat with nonfat cooking spray. Place the pineapple slices on the grill, close the lid, and grill for 3 minutes. Brush the slices with the ginger glaze and serve while warm.

chapter Four

G100™
NORTH AFRICAN & MIDDLE EASTERN FLAVORS!

Moroccan Lemon Chicken | *serves 4*

1 Tbs.	flour
1 tsp.	ground cinnamon
½ tsp.	ground cumin
½ tsp.	ground turmeric
½ tsp.	salt
4	boneless, skinless chicken breasts
1 Tbs.	extra-virgin olive oil
¼ cup	low-sodium chicken broth
	juice of 2 lemons
¼ cup	pitted dates, chopped
¼ cup	toasted almonds, chopped

Combine the flour, cinnamon, cumin, turmeric, and salt, and place with the chicken in a self-sealing plastic bag. Toss well to coat the chicken. Place the Sauté Plate in the grill and preheat to medium-high. Drizzle the olive oil on the Sauté Plate. Add the chicken breasts and close the lid. Cook for 7 to 9 minutes, or until no pink remains and the chicken is cooked through. Add the chicken broth, lemon juice, and pitted dates and simmer together for another 2 minutes. Remove the chicken from the plate onto a serving dish and carefully pour the sauce over all. Garnish with the almonds.

CALORIES:
208

TOTAL FAT:
9g

SATURATED FAT:
<1g

% CAL FROM FAT:
38

CARBOHYDRATES:
14g

PROTEIN:
19g

CHOLESTEROL:
41mg

SODIUM:
338mg

Indian Lamb & Vegetable Kebabs | *serves 4*

CALORIES:
305

TOTAL FAT:
12g

SATURATED FAT:
3g

% CAL FROM FAT:
36

CARBOHYDRATES:
11g

PROTEIN:
37g

CHOLESTEROL:
109mg

SODIUM:
413mg

1½ lbs.	boneless lamb, cut into cubes
1 Tbs.	extra-virgin olive oil
½ tsp.	salt
½ tsp.	freshly ground black pepper
	juice of 1 lemon
1 med.	white onion, peeled and cut into bite-sized wedges
1 large	tomato, cut into bite-sized wedges
1	green bell pepper, seeded and cut into bite-sized squares
1 large	zucchini, cut into 1-inch thick slices
2 Tbs.	plain, lowfat yogurt
12	wooden skewers, soaked in water for 30 minutes

In a large self-sealing bag, combine the lamb, oil, salt, pepper, and lemon juice. Refrigerate for 3 hours or up to 8 hours. Thread the lamb, onion, tomato, bell pepper, and zucchini on the bamboo skewers, alternating equal portions on each skewer. Using a pastry brush, brush the skewered meat and vegetables with the yogurt.

Place the Grilling Plate on the grill and preheat to medium-high. Coat with nonfat cooking spray and place the kebabs on the grill. Close the lid and cook for 6 to 7 minutes, or until the lamb is cooked to your preference.

Tandoori Chicken Kebobs | *serves 4*

CALORIES:
110

TOTAL FAT:
3g

SATURATED FAT:
1g

% CAL FROM FAT:
23

CARBOHYDRATES:
5g

PROTEIN:
15g

CHOLESTEROL:
38mg

SODIUM:
365mg

3	boneless, skinless chicken breasts, cut into bite-sized pieces
1 cup	plain yogurt
¼ tsp.	saffron threads, crushed and dissolved in 1 Tbs. water
1 clove	garlic, minced
1 Tbs.	crushed dried mint
½ tsp.	salt
½ tsp.	freshly ground black pepper
	10 wooden skewers, soaked in water for 30 minutes

In a small bowl, combine all of the ingredients, coating the chicken completely. Cover tightly and refrigerate for at least 2 hours or up to 8 hours.

Place the Grilling Plate on the grill and preheat to medium-high. Coat with nonfat cooking spray. Thread the chicken pieces on the skewers and place on the grill. Close the lid and grill for 6 to 8 minutes, or until the chicken is cooked through and no pink remains.

Lebanese Lamb Steaks | *serves 4*

Great served with grilled eggplant.

2 tsp.	dried oregano
½ tsp.	ground cinnamon
½ tsp.	ground nutmeg
½ tsp.	ground cumin
½ tsp	ground coriander
½ tsp.	smoky paprika
½ tsp.	dried mint
½ tsp.	freshly ground black pepper
½ tsp.	salt
¼ cup	tomato paste
2 tbs.	extra-virgin olive oil
2 cloves	garlic, peeled and minced
4	lamb cutlets, about 6 oz. each

Combine the spices, tomato paste, olive oil, and garlic in a medium bowl. Whisk together thoroughly. Spread the marinade all over the lamb cutlets and refrigerate in a self-sealing plastic bag for at least 3 hours or up to 8 hours.

Place the Grilling Plate on the grill and preheat to medium-high. Coat with nonfat cooking spray and place the lamb cutlets on the grill. Close the lid and grill for 5 to 6 minutes, or until the lamb is cooked to your choice.

CALORIES:
329

TOTAL FAT:
17g

SATURATED FAT:
4g

% CAL FROM FAT:
48

CARBOHYDRATES:
5g

PROTEIN:
37g

CHOLESTEROL:
112mg

SODIUM:
418mg

Baba Ganouj (Eggplant & Sesame Spread) | *serves 4*

2 Tbs.	extra-virgin olive oil, divided
¼ tsp.	salt
3 med.	eggplants, split in half lengthwise
2 Tbs.	tahini (sesame paste)
1 small	white onion, finely chopped
1 Tbs.	flat leaf parsley, minced

In a medium bowl, combine 1 tablespoon of the oil and the salt and spread over the cut sides of each eggplant. Place the Grilling Plate on the grill and preheat to high. Coat with nonfat cooking spray and place the eggplants on the grill, cut-side down. Close the lid and cook for 7 to 8 minutes, or until the eggplants have softened.

Scoop out the eggplant flesh and place in a blender or food processor. Add the tahini and remaining olive oil. Purée until smooth. Place in a serving bowl and sprinkle with onion and parsley. Serve with pita bread for dipping.

CALORIES:
199

TOTAL FAT:
11g

SATURATED FAT:
<1g

% CAL FROM FAT:
46

CARBOHYDRATES:
24g

PROTEIN:
5g

CHOLESTEROL:
0mg

SODIUM:
162mg

Grilled Lemon-Paprika Salmon, North African Style | *serves 4*

½ cup	plain lowfat yogurt
¼ cup	flat leaf parsley, chopped
¼ cup	fresh cilantro, chopped
3 Tbs.	fresh lemon juice
1 Tbs.	extra-virgin olive oil
2 tsp.	ground paprika
1 tsp.	ground cumin
½ tsp.	salt
½ tsp.	freshly ground black pepper
4 6 oz.	salmon fillets

In a medium bowl, combine all of the ingredients except the salmon. Reserve ¼ cup of the yogurt sauce for later use. Place the rest of the sauce in a large, self-sealing plastic bag and add the salmon fillets, coating the salmon well. Refrigerate for 30 minutes.

Place the Grilling Plate on the grill and preheat to high. Coat with nonfat cooking spray. Remove the salmon from the marinade and remove any excess marinade with paper towels. Place the salmon on the grill, close the lid, and grill for 5 minutes, or until the salmon is cooked to your preference. Serve with the reserved yogurt sauce drizzled over the top.

North African Grilled Corn | *serves 4*

1 tsp.	ground cumin
1 tsp.	ground coriander
¼ tsp.	ground ginger
¼ tsp.	ground cinnamon
¼ tsp.	salt
¼ tsp.	freshly ground black pepper
4 small	ears of corn, husks and silk removed
2 Tbs.	lowfat butter-flavored spread, melted

Place the Grill Plate on the grill and preheat to high. In a small bowl, combine the spices. Using a pastry brush, cover the corn with the butter spread. Sprinkle with the spice mixture. Place the corn on the heated grill and close the lid. Grill for 3 minutes. Open the lid and rotate the corn a one-quarter turn. Grill for an additional 3 minutes with the lid closed.

Afghan Kofta Pita Sandwiches | *serves 4*

1 lb.	lean ground beef
¼ cup	soft bread crumbs
1 med.	yellow onion, minced
1	green bell pepper, minced
1 clove	garlic, minced
¼ tsp.	ground coriander
½ tsp.	salt
½ tsp.	freshly ground black pepper
4 fresh	pita breads
½ cup	*Hummus* (p. 54)
16 cherry	tomatoes
1	green bell pepper, cut into bite-sized squares
1 cup	lettuce, shredded
8	wooden skewers, soaked in water for 30 minutes

In a medium bowl, mix the beef, bread crumbs, onion, minced pepper, garlic, coriander, salt, and black pepper until just combined. Form into 16 oval meatballs. Place 2 meatballs on each skewer, along with equal portions of tomatoes and peppers.

Place the Grilling Plate on the grill and preheat to medium-high. Coat with nonfat cooking spray and place the skewers on the grill. Close the lid and grill for 5 to 6 minutes, or until the meat is cooked through. Assemble the sandwiches by dressing the pita bread with *Hummus* and stuffing each with the meatballs, vegetables and lettuce.

CALORIES:
401

TOTAL FAT:
8g

SATURATED FAT:
4g

% CAL FROM FAT:
18

CARBOHYDRATES:
47g

PROTEIN:
34g

CHOLESTEROL:
69mg

SODIUM:
812mg

Grilled Vegetables & Toasted Pita Wedges with Hummus | *serves 4*

CALORIES:
340

TOTAL FAT:
13g

SATURATED FAT:
<1g

% CAL FROM FAT:
33

CARBOHYDRATES:
50g

PROTEIN:
11g

CHOLESTEROL:
0mg

SODIUM:
708mg

2 med.	zucchini, cut lengthwise into ¼-inch slices
2 med.	yellow squash, cut lengthwise into ¼-inch slices
1 large	red bell pepper, stemmed and seeded, cut into 1-inch spears
2 Tbs.	extra-virgin olive oil, divided
2 cloves	garlic, minced
¼ tsp.	salt
¼ tsp.	freshly ground black pepper
4	pita breads, cut into wedges
1 cup	prepared or homemade hummus (recipe follows)

In a large bowl, combine the vegetables, olive oil, garlic, salt, and pepper, until the vegetables are well-coated. Place the Grill Plate on the grill, preheat to high, and coat with the nonfat cooking spray. Working in batches, place the vegetables on the preheated grill, close the lid, and grill for 4 minutes, or until slightly softened. Remove and set aside. Working in batches, place the pita wedges on the grill, close the lid, and grill for 2 minutes, or until toasted. Place a bowl of hummus in the middle of a serving platter and arrange the grilled vegetables and toasted pita wedges around the bowl.

Hummus | *makes about 2 cups*

CALORIES:
180

TOTAL FAT:
9g

SATURATED FAT:
<1g

% CAL FROM FAT:
45

CARBOHYDRATES:
20g

PROTEIN:
6g

CHOLESTEROL:
0mg

SODIUM:
534mg

15½ oz.	can garbanzo beans, undrained
2 Tbs.	tahini (sesame paste)
1 Tbs.	extra-virgin olive oil
1 Tbs.	fresh lemon juice
1 tsp.	ground cumin
½ tsp.	ground coriander
1 clove	garlic, minced
½ tsp.	salt
½ tsp.	crushed red pepper flakes

Place all of the ingredients in a blender or food processor. Process until smooth.

Moroccan Lamb Burgers with Herb Sauce | *serves 4*

1 Tbs.	golden raisins
1 Tbs.	toasted pine nuts
1 Tbs.	flat leaf parsley, chopped
¼ tsp.	ground cumin
¼ tsp.	ground coriander
¼ tsp.	ground cinnamon
1 lb.	ground lamb
4	hamburger buns or pita bread wraps

Yogurt Herb Sauce

1 cup	plain lowfat yogurt
¾ cup	cucumber, peeled and grated
2 cloves	garlic, minced
2 Tbs.	fresh mint leaves, minced
2 Tbs.	fresh lemon juice
¼ tsp.	freshly ground black pepper
¼ tsp.	salt

In a medium bowl, mix the raisins, pine nuts, parsley, cumin, coriander, cinnamon, and ground lamb until just combined. Form into four equal-sized patties. Place the Grilling Plate on the grill and preheat to high. Coat with nonfat cooking spray. Place the burger patties on the grill, close the lid, and grill for 7 minutes, or until cooked to your preference.

Combine the *Yogurt Herb Sauce* ingredients in a medium bowl. To serve, place each patty on a bun or in a pita wrap and dress with the sauce.

CALORIES:
378

TOTAL FAT:
18g

SATURATED FAT:
7g

% CAL FROM FAT:
44

CARBOHYDRATES:
28g

PROTEIN:
25g

CHOLESTEROL:
78mg

SODIUM:
450mg

Moroccan Chicken Kebabs | *serves 4*

CALORIES:
146

TOTAL FAT:
2g

SATURATED FAT:
<1g

% CAL FROM FAT:
9

CARBOHYDRATES:
16g

PROTEIN:
19g

CHOLESTEROL:
41mg

SODIUM:
349mg

1 tsp.	ground cinnamon
½ tsp.	salt
½ tsp.	ground cumin
½ tsp.	ground turmeric
½ tsp.	freshly ground black pepper
1 tsp.	dark brown sugar, packed
4	boneless, skinless chicken breasts, cut into bite-sized pieces
2 small	red onions, peeled and cut into bite-sized wedges
2	green bell peppers, cleaned and cut into bite-sized squares
20	cherry tomatoes
1	lemon, cut into wedges
12	wooden skewers, soaked in water for 30 minutes

In a small bowl, combine the cinnamon, salt, cumin, turmeric, black pepper, and brown sugar. Rub the spices over each piece of chicken and place in a self-sealing plastic bag. Refrigerate for at least 3 hours or overnight.

To make the kebabs, alternate equal portions of the chicken, onion, peppers, and tomatoes on each skewer. Place the Grilling Plate on the grill and preheat to medium-high. Coat with nonfat cooking spray and place the kebabs on the grill. Close the lid and grill for 6 minutes, or until no pink remains and the chicken is cooked through. To serve, spritz each kebab with fresh squeezed lemon juice.

Chapter Five

G100™
NORTH AMERICAN FLAVORS!

California Ball Park Burgers | *makes 4 servings*

1 pound	extra-lean ground beef
1 Tbs.	Worcestershire sauce
1 tsp.	black pepper
1 tsp.	kosher salt
4	hamburger buns

Toppings:
mustard
ketchup
lowfat mayonnaise
horseradish
relish, sweet or dill
lettuce
onion, sliced thin
avocado slices

In a large bowl, thoroughly mix the beef and seasonings together. Shape into 4 patties and set aside. Place the Grilling Plate on the grill and preheat to medium-high. Lightly coat the grill with nonfat cooking spray.

Place the patties on the heated grill. Close the lid and grill for 4 to 5 minutes, or until the patties are cooked through. Place the patties on the buns and add toppings of your choice.

CALORIES:
269

TOTAL FAT:
6g

SATURATED FAT:
4g

% CAL FROM FAT:
22

CARBOHYDRATES:
22g

PROTEIN:
28g

CHOLESTEROL:
69mg

SODIUM:
804mg

Double Turkey & Provolone Burger | *serves 4*

CALORIES:
338

TOTAL FAT:
12g

SATURATED FAT:
7g

% CAL FROM FAT:
30

CARBOHYDRATES:
21g

PROTEIN:
40g

CHOLESTEROL:
80mg

SODIUM:
838mg

1 lb.	ground turkey
½ tsp.	salt
½ tsp.	black pepper
¼ cup	yellow onion, diced
4 slices	turkey bacon
4 slices	part-skim provolone cheese
4	whole-wheat hamburger buns

In a large bowl, thoroughly mix the turkey, salt, pepper and onion together. Shape into 4 patties and set aside. Place the Grilling Plate on the grill and preheat to medium-high. Coat with nonfat cooking spray. Place the turkey bacon on the grill, close the lid and cook for 3 to 4 minutes, or until done. Remove the bacon from the grill and set aside. Place the turkey patties on the heated grill and cook for 6 to 8 minutes until cooked through completely and no pink remains. Place the cheese slices on each of the burgers and continue grilling until the cheese melts over the burger. Place the patties on the buns and top each with the bacon.

Turkey Reuben & Swiss Sandwiches | *serves 4*

CALORIES:
407

TOTAL FAT:
11g

SATURATED FAT:
4g

% CAL FROM FAT:
24

CARBOHYDRATES:
38g

PROTEIN:
43g

CHOLESTEROL:
74mg

SODIUM:
1769mg

1 lb.	ground turkey
½ tsp.	salt
½ tsp.	black pepper
4 Tbs.	lowfat Thousand Island dressing
8 slices	rye bread
4 slices	lowfat Swiss cheese
2 cups	sauerkraut, drained
1 Tbs.	lowfat butter-flavored spread

In a large bowl, thoroughly mix the turkey, salt and pepper together. Shape into 4 patties and set aside. Place the Grilling Plate on the grill and preheat to medium-high. Coat with nonfat cooking spray. Place the turkey patties on the heated grill. Close the lid and grill for 6 to 8 minutes, or until the patties are cooked through completely and no pink remains.

Spread the dressing on each slice of bread. Place the 4 patties on 4 slices of bread, add 1 slice of cheese and mound ½ cup of sauerkraut on top of each. Cover the sandwiches with the remaining pieces of bread. Lightly cover the outside of each piece of bread with the butter spread. Place 2 sandwiches on the grill and cook until the cheese is slightly melted and the fillings are warm. Repeat with the remaining 2 sandwiches.

Southwestern-Style Steak Fajitas | *serves 4*

1 tsp.	garlic powder
1 tsp.	chili powder
½ tsp.	salt
1½ lbs.	beef sirloin, thinly sliced
1 med.	yellow onion, peeled and thinly sliced
1 red	bell pepper, seeded and thinly sliced
1 Tbs.	cilantro, chopped

Prepare the Sauté Plate on the grill and preheat the grill to high. Coat with nonfat cooking spray. Combine the garlic powder, chili powder and salt in a small bowl. Season the beef with the spices. Place the beef, onion and bell pepper on the grill and close the lid. Cook for 3 to 4 minutes, or until the beef has cooked through and the vegetables have softened. Garnish with the chopped cilantro. Serve with corn tortillas, rice, and beans.

CALORIES:
254

TOTAL FAT:
9g

SATURATED FAT:
3g

% CAL FROM FAT:
32

CARBOHYDRATES:
5g

PROTEIN:
37g

CHOLESTEROL:
104mg

SODIUM:
398mg

Grilled Paprika Chicken Thighs | *serves 6*

1 tsp.	ground cumin
1 Tbs.	ground paprika
1 small	white onion, peeled and chopped
5 cloves	garlic, peeled and chopped
2½ Tbs.	fresh lemon juice
2 Tbs.	extra-virgin olive oil
½ tsp.	salt
½ tsp.	freshly ground black pepper
1 cup	plain lowfat yogurt
12	boneless chicken thighs

Place the cumin, paprika, onion, garlic, lemon juice, olive oil, salt, pepper, and yogurt in a food processor or blender. Process until smooth. Place the marinade in a self-sealing plastic bag with the chicken thighs and coat the thighs thoroughly. Refrigerate for at least 3 hours or up to 8 hours.

Place the Grilling Plate on the grill and preheat to medium-high. Coat with nonfat cooking spray and place the chicken on grill. Close the lid and grill for 7 to 9 minutes, or until the chicken is cooked through and no pink remains.

CALORIES:
330

TOTAL FAT:
23g

SATURATED FAT:
5g

% CAL FROM FAT:
63

CARBOHYDRATES:
8g

PROTEIN:
22g

CHOLESTEROL:
98mg

SODIUM:
311mg

Southwestern-style Omelet | serves 2

CALORIES: 221

TOTAL FAT: 14g

SATURATED FAT: 6g

% CAL FROM FAT: 57

CARBOHYDRATES: 4g

PROTEIN: 20g

CHOLESTEROL: 346mg

SODIUM: 524mg

3	eggs (or egg substitute equivalent)
2 Tbs.	canned diced green chilies
2	green onions, finely sliced
¼ cup	lowfat cheddar cheese, shredded
¼ cup	mesquite smoked turkey, diced

Place the Sauté Plate on the grill and preheat to medium. Coat with nonfat cooking spray.

In a medium bowl, beat together the eggs. Add the green chilies and onions, and mix well to combine. Pour the egg mixture on the Plate, making sure the entire plate is covered. In the center, place the cheddar cheese and diced turkey. Close the lid and cook for 3 minutes. Using a plastic spatula, fold over one side of cooked egg to form the omelet. Cut in half before serving.

Grilled Asparagus with Balsamic Glaze | makes 4 servings

CALORIES: 59

TOTAL FAT: 4g

SATURATED FAT: <1g

% CAL FROM FAT: 50

CARBOHYDRATES: 6g

PROTEIN: 3g

CHOLESTEROL: 0mg

SODIUM: 148mg

1 lb.	fresh asparagus, trimmed
1 Tbs.	extra-virgin olive oil
¼ tsp.	salt
1 Tbs.	balsamic vinegar

In a medium bowl, combine the asparagus, olive oil, and salt, until the asparagus is evenly coated.

Place the Grilling Plate on the grill and preheat to high. Coat with nonfat cooking spray. Place the asparagus on the preheated grill, close the lid, and cook for 3 minutes. Open the lid and drizzle balsamic vinegar over the asparagus. Close the lid and cook for another minute.

Grilled Chicken Caesar Salad | *serves 4*

3	boneless, skinless chicken breasts
2 Tbs.	extra-virgin olive oil, divided
2 Tbs.	fresh lemon juice
4 cloves	garlic, minced
1 Tbs.	fresh parsley, chopped
¼ tsp.	salt
¼ tsp.	freshly ground black pepper
2 heads	romaine lettuce, cut in half lengthwise
¼ tsp.	salt
¼ tsp.	freshly ground black pepper
2 oz.	Parmesan cheese, grated
½ cup	lowfat croutons
¼ cup	reduced-fat Caesar dressing

In a self-sealing plastic bag, combine the chicken with 1 tablespoon of the oil, lemon juice, garlic, parsley, salt, and pepper. Refrigerate for 1 hour or up to 8 hours.

Place the Grilling Plate on the grill and preheat to high. Coat with nonfat cooking spray. Place the chicken on the grill, close the lid, and cook for 7 to 9 minutes, or until the chicken is cooked through and no pink remains. Cool and cut into strips.

Meanwhile, season the lettuce with the remaining oil, salt, and pepper. Place the lettuce, cut-side down, on the grill (on high heat) and cook for 2 minutes, or until the lettuce has softened. Remove from the grill and place on a serving platter. Top each romaine half with sliced chicken, Parmesan cheese, croutons, and Caesar dressing.

CALORIES:
253

TOTAL FAT:
16g

SATURATED FAT:
4g

% CAL FROM FAT:
57

CARBOHYDRATES:
8g

PROTEIN:
19g

CHOLESTEROL:
44mg

SODIUM:
755mg

Grilled Artichokes with Garlic Aioli | *makes 4 servings*

2 med.	artichokes, cleaned and trimmed
1 Tbs.	extra-virgin olive oil
½ tsp.	salt
½ tsp.	freshly ground black pepper
1 cup	*Garlic Aioli* (see recipe on p. 10)

Steam the artichokes for 15 minutes. They will not be fully cooked. While the artichokes are steaming, place the Grilling Plate on the grill and preheat to medium-high. Coat with nonfat cooking spray. Cut the artichokes in half, lengthwise, and season with olive oil, salt, and pepper. Place the artichokes halves cut side down on the grill, close the lid, and cook for 10 minutes. Remove from grill and serve with *Garlic Aioli* for dipping.

CALORIES:
69

TOTAL FAT:
4g

SATURATED FAT:
<1g

% CAL FROM FAT:
42

CARBOHYDRATES:
9g

PROTEIN:
3g

CHOLESTEROL:
0mg

SODIUM:
367mg

Grilled Portobello Mushrooms with Blue Cheese & Walnuts | *makes 8 appetizer servings*

CALORIES:
75

TOTAL FAT:
7g

SATURATED FAT:
2g

% CAL FROM FAT:
76

CARBOHYDRATES:
1g

PROTEIN:
3g

CHOLESTEROL:
8mg

SODIUM:
222mg

4 large	Portobello mushrooms, cleaned and stems removed
1 Tbs.	extra-virgin olive oil
¼ tsp.	salt
¼ tsp.	freshly ground black pepper
3 oz.	blue cheese, crumbled
3 Tbs.	walnuts, chopped
1 Tbs.	fresh flat leaf parsley, minced
1 Tbs.	balsamic vinegar

In a medium bowl, combine the mushrooms, olive oil, salt, and pepper, until the mushrooms are evenly coated.

Place the Grilling Plate on the grill and preheat to high. Coat with nonfat cooking spray. Place the mushrooms on the grill, rib side up, and close the lid. Cook for 3 minutes, or until the mushrooms have softened. Open the lid, drizzle the mushrooms with balsamic vinegar, and sprinkle with the blue cheese and walnuts. Close the lid and cook for another minute. Remove from the grill and cut into wedges for appetizer servings. Sprinkle with parsley.

Dijon Dill Salmon | *makes 4 servings*

CALORIES:
241

TOTAL FAT:
10g

SATURATED FAT:
<1g

% CAL FROM FAT:
39

CARBOHYDRATES:
2g

PROTEIN:
35g

CHOLESTEROL:
89mg

SODIUM:
458mg

2 ½ Tbs.	Dijon mustard
2 Tbs.	fresh dill, minced
1 Tbs.	extra-virgin olive oil
1 Tbs.	fresh lemon juice
½ tsp.	salt
½ tsp.	freshly ground black pepper
4 6 oz.	boneless salmon fillets

In a small bowl, whisk the mustard, dill, olive oil, lemon juice, salt, and pepper. Pour this mixture over the salmon fillets and refrigerate for 1 hour.

Place the Grilling Plate on the grill and preheat to high. Coat with nonfat cooking spray. Remove the salmon from the marinade and place on the heated grill. Close the lid and grill for 4 minutes, or until the salmon is cooked through.

Vineyard Chicken Wraps | *makes 4 servings*

2	boneless, skinless chicken breasts
	salt & pepper to taste
2 tsp.	fresh lemon juice
2 Tbs.	fresh tarragon, minced
3 Tbs.	reduced-fat mayonnaise
¼ tsp.	salt
¼ tsp.	freshly ground black pepper
2 stalks	celery, sliced
	about 20 red seedless grapes, halved
½ cup	toasted pecans, chopped
2 large	flour tortillas

Place the Grilling Plate on the grill and preheat to high. Coat with nonfat cooking spray. Season the chicken breasts with salt and pepper to taste and place the chicken breasts on the preheated grill. Close the lid and cook for 7 to 9 minutes or until the chicken is cooked through and no pink remains. Remove from the grill and set aside to rest for 5 minutes. Cut the chicken into small bite-sized pieces.

In a small bowl, combine the lemon juice, tarragon, mayonnaise, salt, and pepper, whisking together until smooth. In a large bowl, combine the chicken pieces, celery, grapes, and pecans, and dress with the mayonnaise mixture. Place one-half of the mixture in the middle of each tortilla and roll up to create a wrap. Bias-cut the wrap into two pieces.

CALORIES:
310

TOTAL FAT:
15g

SATURATED FAT:
2g

% CAL FROM FAT:
42

CARBOHYDRATES:
32g

PROTEIN:
14g

CHOLESTEROL:
21mg

SODIUM:
504mg

Grilled Strawberry Breakfast Croissants | *serves 4*

¼ cup	lowfat ricotta cheese
¼ cup	reduced-fat cream cheese, softened
½ cup	strawberry preserves
4 large	croissant rolls, cut in half horizontally

In a medium bowl, combine the ricotta cheese, cream cheese, and strawberry preserves until well-mixed. Divide into 8 portions and spread onto each croissant half. Place the croissant halves together.

Place the Grilling Plate on the grill and preheat to medium-high. Coat with nonfat cooking spray. Place the croissant sandwiches on the grill and close the lid. Grill for 2 to 3 minutes, or until the cheese and strawberries are warm and slightly melted.

CALORIES:
432

TOTAL FAT:
18g

SATURATED FAT:
10g

% CAL FROM FAT:
38

CARBOHYDRATES:
55g

PROTEIN:
9g

CHOLESTEROL:
59mg

SODIUM:
599mg

Grilled Peaches | *makes 4 servings*

2 med.	ripe, but firm peaches, pitted and halved
1 Tbs.	brown sugar, packed
1 tsp.	ground cinnamon
4 scoops	vanilla ice cream or frozen yogurt

Place the Grilling Plate on the grill and preheat to high. Coat with nonfat cooking spray. Sprinkle the cut-side of the peaches with the brown sugar and cinnamon. Place the peaches, cut-side down, on the grill, close the lid and grill for 3 minutes. Remove from the grill and serve with a scoop of ice cream cradled in the middle of each.

CALORIES: 166
TOTAL FAT: 3g
SATURATED FAT: 2g
% CAL FROM FAT: 15
CARBOHYDRATES: 33g
PROTEIN: 4g
CHOLESTEROL: 10mg
SODIUM: 102mg

Grilled Balsamic Strawberry Kabobs | *serves 4*

20	ripe, but firm large strawberries, cored
1 Tbs.	balsamic vinegar
4	wooden skewers, soaked in water for 30 minutes

Place 5 strawberries on each skewer. Place the Grilling Plate on the grill and preheat to high. Coat with nonfat cooking spray. Place the kabobs on grill, close the lid, and cook for 2 minutes. Open the lid and drizzle the kabobs with balsamic vinegar. Cook for another minute. Remove from the grill.

CALORIES: 86
TOTAL FAT: 1g
SATURATED FAT: <1g
% CAL FROM FAT: 9
CARBOHYDRATES: 20g
PROTEIN: 2g
CHOLESTEROL: 0mg
SODIUM: 3mg